ASTD Training Basics Series

FACILITATION
Basics

DONALD V. McCAIN
DEBORAH D. TOBEY

A Complete How-to Guide to Help You:

Enhance Your Skills as a Facilitator

Create Supportive and Effective Learning Environments

Ensure Learning Is Transferred to the Job

ASTD Press

ASTD Press is an internationally renowned source of insightful and practical information on workplace learning and performance topics, including training basics, evaluation and return-on-investment (ROI), instructional systems development (ISD), e-learning, leadership, and career development.

Ordering information: Books published by ASTD Press can be purchased by visiting our website at store.astd.org or by calling 800.628.2783 or 703.683.8100.

Library of Congress Control Number: 2003113722

ISBN-13: 978-1-56286-361-6
ISBN-10: 1-56286-361-4

Acquisitions and Development Editor: Mark Morrow
Copyeditor: Karen Eddleman
Interior Design and Production: Kathleen Schaner
Cover Design: Ana Ilieva
Cover Illustration: Phil and Jim Bliss

Table of Contents

About the
Training Basics Series

■ ■

A STD's *Training Basics* series recognizes and, in some ways, celebrates the fast-paced, ever-changing reality of organizations today. Jobs, roles, and expectations change quickly. One day you might be a network administrator or a process line manager, and the next day you might be asked to train 50 employees in basic computer skills or to instruct line workers in quality processes.

Where do you turn for help? The ASTD *Training Basics* series is designed to be your one-stop solution. The series takes a minimalist approach to your learning curve dilemma and presents only the information you need to be successful. Each book in the series guides you through key aspects of training: giving presentations, making the transition to the role of trainer, designing and delivering training, and evaluating training. The books in the series also include some advanced skills such as performance and basic business proficiencies.

The ASTD *Training Basics* series is the perfect tool for training and performance professionals looking for easy-to-understand materials that will prepare non-trainers to take on a training role. In addition, this series is the perfect reference tool for any trainer's bookshelf and a quick way to hone your existing skills. The titles in the series include:

- ▶ *Presentation Basics*
- ▶ *Trainer Basics*
- ▶ *Training Design Basics*
- ▶ *Facilitation Basics*
- ▶ *Communication Basics*

Preface

So, you are now the teacher, instructor, trainer, the person who will be leading a class of adult learners. In other words, you're now a facilitator of learning experiences. Where do you go from here? You may not know it, but you've already embarked on the journey to becoming a great facilitator! The mere fact that you're reading this book means that you have already discovered that facilitating learning is *not* the same thing as presenting information (but more on that as we go along). That's key to your success.

What Is a Facilitator, Anyway?

The expression, "Those who can, do; and those who can't, teach," could not be farther off the mark. The fact is that those who teach, or facilitate learning, and do it well know their subjects (both content and application of that content to the job) better than anyone else.

Subject matter expertise is the foundation for facilitating an effective learning experience. Furthermore, facilitation proficiency—the focus of this book—is a new skill set that supports your ability to facilitate others' learning and application of the subject matter.

The word *facilitate* comes from the Latin word, *facilis*, which means "to make easy." As facilitators, that is our job: to guide the learning process and make the journey as smooth and as rewarding as possible for our learners—to make the learning easy.

Who Should Read This Book?

We have written this book for people who want to enhance their skills in facilitating others' learning experiences in an organizational environment. That group might include

▶ subject matter experts who occasionally function in a training role or who are moving into a training role in their jobs

- ▶ trainers who are ready to move beyond presenting information or using learning activities for their entertainment value only
- ▶ faculty members in educational institutions who want to add skill and application to their classroom experiences
- ▶ HR professionals or managers who contract with facilitators and want to evaluate their performance
- ▶ trainers who want to enhance their facilitation skills
- ▶ trainers whose organizations are holding the training function accountable for learners' performance back on the job.

Our purpose in this book is to facilitate your learning and assist in enhancing your facilitation skills. When you continue your learning journey by enhancing your own skills, you will increase the learning that takes place in your courses, increase the probability of skill transfer back to your learners' jobs, and increase the impact of training on your organization.

Chapter-by-Chapter Highlights

Your success as a facilitator of learning depends on your ability to immerse yourself in the learning experience with the learners by sharing it with them and guiding them at the same time. Your success also depends on creating an environment that is safe for the learners on multiple levels (interpersonal, physical, psychological, and emotional).

Each chapter focuses on a critical aspect of creating and maintaining an optimal learning environment. Here's a summary of the 10 chapters in *Facilitation Basics:*

1. "Introduction: It's Not About You! It's About Them!" gives you an overview of the book. It establishes the premise that effective facilitation is about the learners, not about the facilitator. Finally, some considerations are discussed that will help you appraise the course design in preparation for facilitation.
2. "Learning Facilitation" presents the principles that underlie effective learning facilitation and explains why effective learning is about the learners. The chapter covers the differences between presenting and facilitating, how adults learn, and the implications for facilitation of learning.
3. "Learner and Facilitator" focuses on learner preferences and learning styles, what it takes to be a facilitator, roles that learning facilitators take on, and criteria for selecting effective facilitators.

4. "Getting Started" builds on a premise of this book: that it is critical to focus on what happens in the learning environment as the learning unfolds. To start a learning session off on the right foot means the facilitator must know the audience, create a climate for learning, establish a physical presence, and personalize learning materials.

5. "Facilitating Learning Activities" discusses the types of learning activities used by facilitators, the goals of these learning activities, and the planning that must be done before you ever get in front of the learner group.

6. "Facilitation Techniques" addresses the events that occur as the learning experience unfolds, along with how to facilitate those events, including the sequencing of activities, giving activity instructions, managing time, managing group size, grouping participants, monitoring activities, providing feedback, managing assessments and measurements, and adjusting facilitation on the fly.

7. "Managing Difficult Participants" offers techniques for working with difficult participants, starting with the idea that perhaps defining them as "difficult" is part of the problem! Considerable time is spent looking at ways that facilitators can set aside personal agendas and focus on the professional agenda, which is to make learning happen. To support this, tactics to handle disruptive behavior, both prior to and during the learning experience, are identified and described.

8. "Using Media to Support Learning" introduces the world of media available to you as a facilitator. Believe it or not, there really is a whole world outside of Microsoft PowerPoint! In this chapter, using media specifically to support the identified learning needs is discussed (and there are appropriate situations for PowerPoint). Tips for using each type of media effectively are presented as well.

9. "Assessing Facilitation Quality" covers ways facilitators can get feedback on their performance and ways that facilitator quality (either your own or a facilitator you manage) can be assessed using materials that are built into your courses, such as tests, assessments, and smile sheets.

10. "A Final Note" can help you pull everything together. In this chapter, food for thought is presented on the facilitator's role in the organization.

In addition, the book includes an Additional Resources section that lists many sources to support your professional growth as a facilitator.

Icons to Guide You

This book strives to make it as easy as possible for you to understand and apply its lessons. Icons throughout the book help you identify key points that can mean the difference between a facilitation success or an embarrassment.

What's Inside This Chapter?

Each chapter opens with a short summary for quick reference to what's in that chapter. You can use this section to identify the information in the chapter, and, if you wish, to skip ahead to the material that is most useful.

Think About This

These are helpful tips that you can pull out of your hip pocket to help prepare for facilitation or during facilitation.

Basic Rules

These rules cut to the chase. They are unequivocal and important concepts for facilitators.

Noted

This icon is used to give you more detail or explanation about a concept or a principle. Sometimes it is used for a short but productive tangent.

Getting It Done

The final section of each chapter supports your ability to take the content of that chapter and apply it to your situation. Sometimes this section contains a list of questions for you to ponder; sometimes it is a self-assessment tool; and sometimes it is a list of action steps you can take to enhance your facilitation.

Acknowledgments

We dedicate this book to our spouses, Kathy McCain and Bryan Tobey, and our families, who supported us through this endeavor. We also thank our many peers who dialogued with us and gave us feedback.

Donald V. McCain
Deborah Davis Tobey
March 2004

1
Introduction: It's Not About You— It's About Them!

■ ■

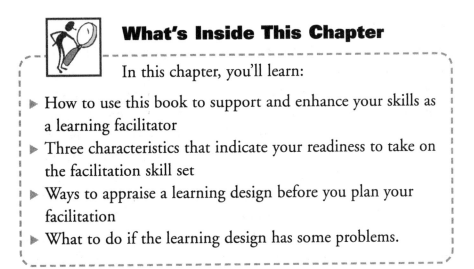

What's Inside This Chapter

In this chapter, you'll learn:

▶ How to use this book to support and enhance your skills as a learning facilitator

▶ Three characteristics that indicate your readiness to take on the facilitation skill set

▶ Ways to appraise a learning design before you plan your facilitation

▶ What to do if the learning design has some problems.

How *Facilitation Basics* Can Help You

Facilitating a learning experience can be extremely rewarding, but it is also a challenge. The reward for facilitators comes from the learners: their success when they learn content; use and apply it; grow; and, ultimately, perform better back on the job. It's a great feeling to watch people's faces light up when they master a new concept!

The challenge for facilitators comes from the same source as the reward: from the learners. Facilitating learning experiences is about the learners. The focus must be on the learners at all times. For those whose background is in presentations and in content expertise, this is a new paradigm. Many presenters and trainers are used to focusing on themselves and their preparedness for questions, control of the group, and expertise.

Basic Rule 1
It's always about the learners!

Some Assumptions

This book necessarily begins with some assumptions about characteristics and skills that you already possess. Your work with this book will be based on these assumptions:

- ▶ *Assumption 1:* You already possess basic platform skills: You are comfortable in front of a group, and you have mastered the principles of basic presentation techniques, including stance, voice, gestures, eye contact, and basic media skills. This book will help you review and build on those skills.
- ▶ *Assumption 2:* You are an expert in the subject matter you are facilitating. This means you have thorough knowledge and experience in the subject area and can share examples, stories, and your rich background with learners to enhance your facilitation.
- ▶ *Assumption 3:* You have a well-designed course to facilitate. Learning design and facilitation go hand-in-hand in making an effective learning experience. Although the focus is in this book is on the facilitation aspect, you must first appraise the training design that you have been given.

If your situation is not reflected in the first assumption, you may wish to consider some additional practice on your presentation skills until you feel comfortable with that skill set. Another book in this series, *Presentation Basics* (Rosania, 2003), as well as the other publications listed in the Additional Resources section can help you hone your presentation skills.

If you need to increase your subject matter expertise, try getting more experience and practice, or shadow an expert. Another alternative is to partner with a subject matter expert who can co-facilitate a learning experience with you.

If the course you are to facilitate has an incomplete design or some design problems, you may need to assess the need for, and, if necessary, do some prework to enhance the design before facilitating the course. Design considerations are addressed in some detail in the next section.

Before You Begin: Design Considerations

As a facilitator, you will be handicapped from the start if the original course design isn't effective. Depending on the situation, enhancing the design before you start can be an effective option. You must review the needs assessment findings, check the learning objectives, and make sure that the learning activities and assessment/measurement methods align with the learning objectives.

> **Think About This**
>
> The three main design components that you must investigate, appraise, and perhaps enhance before beginning to facilitate a course are:
> - *learner profile information:* available, detailed, and accurate
> - *learning objectives:* alignment with learning activities and measurements/assessments
> - *content segmentation and flow:* must-know content is clear; flow and segmentation support effective learning.

Needs Assessment Findings

Your course designer, facilitator guide, course materials, and your client should provide you with needs assessment information regarding the learners' backgrounds, skill levels, learning styles, comfort with learning activities, work environments, and attitudes toward the learning experience. Knowing the audience profile will enhance your facilitation to a great extent and enable you to customize your facilitation to the learners' characteristics and needs.

Learning Objectives

Learning objectives and outcomes should be specified and should be stated in observable, measurable terms. With specific and measurable learning objectives, you will always have in mind

Noted

You'll notice the word client used frequently throughout this book. In this context, your client is defined as "the person who benefits from the increased job performance of your learners." Usually, the client is the learners' manager(s).

where you are "driving" the learning and what the learners must be able to do when your course is complete and they are back on their jobs.

The course content should be segmented appropriately for learning effectiveness (not too much content at one time without practice and application). The must-know content should be clearly identified in the participant materials and handouts for your benefit as well as the learners'.

Activities and Assessments

Learning activities and assessment/measurement methods should align with the learning objectives they represent. In this way, the course design ensures that your learners' experiences will result in the learning that is required and increase the probability of their transferring the skills back to their jobs.

The design should also encompass a variety of types of learning activities and a varied pace. Learning activity sequence should be varied as well: The principle is that activities must appeal to all learning styles and knowledge/skill levels at some point or another in the learning experience. In addition, the type of knowledge or skills assessment and measurement should align with the stated learning objectives.

Noted

Effective learning is the result of both effective design and facilitation, and it is acknowledged that the line dividing the two areas of expertise is not a clear-cut delineation. Effective design supports effective facilitation, and there will be times when that dividing line is pushed a bit to discuss or acknowledge the design implications of a particular area of facilitation. This book is not intended to teach you how to design (or redesign) training, although that is the focus of another title in this series: Training Design Basics *(Carliner, 2003).*

Making Do With a Suboptimal or Incomplete Design

What if the course design and materials that you have been given do not contain all the components of good learning design? Depending on the situation, you have a few options:

▶ Go back to the course designer and ask for a redesign to include these components.

▶ Work in tandem with the course designer to rework the design.

▶ Interview the course designer to obtain the necessary information and build it into the facilitation yourself.

▶ Go with what you have and hope for the best. This is not the best course of action and typically results in lower quality of results. Although a good facilitator can make a seminar or workshop fun, it takes both a well-thought-out design and excellent facilitation skills to produce a high-quality learning experience.

Ready, Set, Go!

So . . . if facilitating isn't about the design of learning before the course begins, what is it about?

It's about what happens during the learning experience itself. It's about meeting the learners where they are, not where you are. It's about letting the learners have the first crack at the learning (self-discovery) so that it belongs to them, not you. It's about understanding that the learning experience is about their mastering and applying knowledge and skills; it's not about how much content you can cover in the time allotted.

To enhance your learning about facilitation, you will be provided with examples, worksheets, checklists, and other tools to aid you in thinking through your own facilitation of learning and to help you make these principles and concepts yours.

Ready to get started?

 ### Getting It Done

In this first chapter, you learned about the three characteristics that you must have before you can effectively facilitate a learning event. The chapter also discussed how to appraise a learning design and what to do if it falls short. Exercise 1-1 will aid you in assessing your readiness and the readiness of the learning design that you have been given.

Exercise 1-1. Are you ready?

In Section 1, indicate your readiness as a facilitator by checking the "Yes/No" column and adding details in the "Comments" column. For those items that you would like to develop further, jot your plans and ideas in the "Action Items" column. Then, in Section 2, indicate the adequacy of the learning design by checking the "Yes/No" column, adding details in the "Comments" column. Itemize your plans to improve the design (if any) in the "Action Items" column.

Section 1: Facilitator Readiness

Item	Yes	No	Comments	Action Items
I am confident of my basic presentation skills: • Stance • Voice • Gestures • Eye contact • Basic media skills				
I am confident of my expertise in the subject matter of the course I am to facilitate: • Knowledge • Experience • Examples • Stories				

Section 2: Learning Design Appraisal

Item	Yes	No	Comments	Action Items
Needs assessment information on the learners is available, detailed, and accurate: • Backgrounds • Skill levels • Learning styles • Comfort with learning activities • Work environments • Attitudes toward the learning experience				

Section 2: Learning Design Appraisal (continued)

Item	Yes	No	Comments	Action Items
Learning objectives are appropriate: • Specific • Aligned with learning activities and measurements/ assessments • Stated in observable, measurable terms				
Content segmentation and flow are clear and support effective learning: • Segmented appropriately • Must-know content is clearly identified • Variety of types of learning activities • Varied pace and learning activity sequence				

In chapter 2, your focus will be on how facilitators are differentiated from presenters and on the implications for learning facilitation that are inherent in the art and science of how adults learn.

2

Learning Facilitation

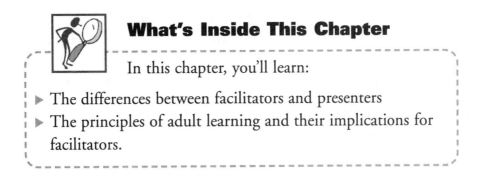

What's Inside This Chapter

In this chapter, you'll learn:

▶ The differences between facilitators and presenters
▶ The principles of adult learning and their implications for facilitators.

Facilitator or Presenter: What's the Difference?

The purpose of learning facilitation is to guide the learners to agreed-upon destinations, which are the learning outcomes. As such, facilitating a learning experience is like being a guide on a jungle safari: You point people in the right direction, make suggestions, take steps to enhance the experience for the participants, and give guidance—but you don't do it *for* them. In fact, you do it *with* them. It would be a poor safari guide who gives the participants a map, says, "Have a great trip," and then sits back in a lawn chair to watch. The same is true of a learning facilitator.

One hallmark of true facilitation is that facilitators, to the extent possible, do not separate themselves from the learner audience; they are with the learners in the experience all the way. The facilitator is one of them, yet not one of them, and guides them to the learning destination.

The facilitator is responsible and accountable to the group; therefore, the facilitator's role is one of earned trust and honor. It's a different role from a teacher/instructor/presenter in a classroom, where there is a clear and obvious separation between the learners and the presenter, and in which the presenter is positioned as an expert who knows all. The learners are merely passive recipients of the knowledge. The facilitator knows the subject area, absolutely, but more than that, the facilitator is concerned with helping the learners know and apply the subject matter. The facilitator's goal is not simply to inform, but to equip the learners for self-development and growth, for continual learning about the subject to the point of mastery.

Three main characteristics differentiate facilitators from presenters: focus, control, and credibility. Each of these characteristics of facilitators is discussed in the sections that follow.

Focus

With facilitation, the focus is on the learner. When you observe both a presentation and a facilitated learning event, many obvious differences appear. One of the most important differences, however, is one that is not visible: the focus.

In a presentation, the focus is on the presenter. All the materials, the presenter's behaviors, and the actions are centered on the presenter. The goals for the presentation are to cover the material and to showcase the presenter's expertise and skill. Conversely, in a facilitated learning event, the focus is on the learner. All of the materials, the facilitator's behaviors, and the activities are centered on helping the learners learn and apply the content. The goal here is simple and profound: Make the learning and application happen.

Control

Facilitators share control. A presenter presents information or content to the audience. A good presenter has excellent command of language and vocabulary, an engaging speaking style, and a command of the subject. By definition, an excellent

Basic Rule 2
Facilitation is learner-centered; presentations are presenter-centered.

presentation results in the audience being informed about the subject matter and taking away useful information.

Because the presentation centers on the presenter, that person is in control of the subject and how the audience engages with the subject (or not). The presenter decides when questions are allowed, and which questions to address. Most of the action is on the part of the presenter; the audience remains largely passive. By exercising this control, the presenter takes on full responsibility for the audience's increase in knowledge. And, by simply presenting information to learners without providing opportunities for them to engage with it, practice it, apply it, and make it their own, the presenter is essentially handing over a map, saying "Have a great trip!" and letting the learners find the way on their own. There's no guarantee that the learners will use the information or learn from it.

For a facilitator, content expertise and presentation skills are the threshold, the beginning, the proverbial foot in the door for a learning experience. Without these two ingredients, the potential facilitator is not even considered for the job. Effective facilitation, however, only begins with content expertise and presentation skills. An effective facilitator gives up much of the control of the content to the learner audience and shares responsibility for the learning with the learner audience. As the guide, the facilitator establishes the climate, learning structure, and flow of the learning.

The learners have a great deal of flexibility in asking and responding to questions, engaging the facilitator and peer learners in discussion, and applying the content to their jobs. Because control is jointly held between the facilitator and the learners, so, too, is accountability for learning. Not being passive, the learners have accountability to both learn and apply the content as the facilitator guides the learning and application.

As the learners gain more control, the facilitator must increasingly use listening, questioning, and coaching skills to build on the learners' experiences as they engage and apply the content. Is this harder than being a presenter? You bet it is! Presentation occurs at the thinking level. Facilitation occurs at multiple levels: thinking, feeling, intuitive, physical, synergistic, and emotional—all of which the facilitator must respond to, keep track of, and invite learner involvement in as the learning event proceeds. And the paradox is, the more control that is given to the learners, the more real learning occurs.

Credibility

Facilitators derive credibility from more than subject matter expertise. Presenters gain (or lose) credibility in the minds of the audience from the content of the presentation, from their mastery of that content, and by their ability to relate the content to their relevant experience. The presenter's ability to give examples, tell war stories, and answer questions from a strong background and experience results in "expert" credibility. But, what happens if a presenter doesn't know the answer to a question? Or, when the presenter's answer and the learner's experiences aren't in sync, and the learner rejects the answer? Credibility in the eyes of the audience is damaged or even disappears.

Whereas content expertise and control provide credibility for presenters, what facilitators do with these components is what creates credibility for them. Facilitator credibility derives from the ability to create and sustain a supportive learning environment and link the learning to the learners' jobs. It comes from the facilitator's interpersonal handling of the group process, keeping the spotlight on the learners. It comes from the ability to be flexible and adjust the content to the learners' needs in the moment. It is how the facilitator engages the learners and helps them to self-discover the learning. It comes from the facilitator's efforts to support the learning, rather than solely from the facilitator's subject matter expertise.

In this way, when the facilitator is asked a question that he or she can't answer (a rare event, of course!), he or she facilitates the group's finding of the answer together, and by doing so, retains and even increases credibility. Alternatively, if the facilitator does not know the answer, he or she has the confidence to say, "I don't know, but I'll find out" without damaging credibility.

Noted

A facilitator focuses on the learners, whereas a presenter focuses on self and the content. A facilitator shares control of the session and the environment with the learners, but a presenter controls all facets. A facilitator derives credibility from subject matter expertise, presentation skills, interpersonal skills, questioning skills, management of the learning environment, sharing of ideas, flexibility, and linkage of learning to the learners' experiences and jobs, while a presenter derives credibility solely from subject matter expertise and presentation skills.

Principles of Adult Learning

The term *adult learning* has two aspects: adult and learning. What do these really mean in relationship to helping adults learn?

First take a look at the word *adult*. When do people become adults? Is it when they become 18? Is it when they enter high school or college? Is it when they take on the responsibilities of a job or family? From a learning perspective, people are adults when they become self-directing, and when they accept responsibility for their own lives. As an adult, being self-directed becomes an important component of one's self-concept.

Learning is somewhat easier to define. According to Nadler and Nadler (1994), "Learning is the acquisition of new skills, attitudes, and knowledge." Learning results in change. For facilitation effectiveness, the emphasis must be on both the acquisition and use of the new knowledge, skills, attitudes, and abilities.

Facilitation is the art of bringing adults together with the learning, by helping adults learn through self-discovery. Facilitation involves techniques for learners to learn from each other in the sharing of knowledge and experiences.

Mitchell indicates that there are basic or foundational principles of adult education. He discusses these principles in some detail in his 1998 book, *The Trainer's Handbook*. By keeping these principles in mind, you can more easily identify with the adult learner and provide meaningful learning experiences for him or her. Adult learning principles provide a framework for development and facilitation that helps ensure the desired results. Mitchell's principles of adult learning are introduced here.

 Noted

In the early 1970s Malcolm Knowles introduced to the United States the term andragogy, *meaning "the art and science of how adults learn" and contrasted it with* pedagogy, *the teaching of children (Knowles, 1990). The mission of education, according to Knowles is "to produce competent people—people who are able to apply their knowledge under changing conditions; and we know that the foundational competence all people must have is the competence to engage in lifelong self-directed learning . . . . The way to produce competent people is to have them acquire their knowledge in the context of its application" (Knowles, 1988).*

Readiness to Learn

Learner readiness is critical to success. Without learner readiness, there is resistance, and learning does not take place. The facilitator should encourage the participant to discuss openly his or her resistance. Once the nature of the resistance is understood, it can be addressed. (See chapter 7 for more on different kinds of learner resistance.)

One of the indicators for adult readiness to learn is when adults face situations requiring them to use the new knowledge, skills, or abilities. Timing, therefore, can be an important consideration. For example, if people are being trained on a new system or product that won't be available for four months, the learner is not ready to learn. This situation happens quite frequently. The facilitator must position the content as a requirement for success in the near future. It's important, too, for the facilitator to be available for follow-up, coaching, or a refresher course at the right time.

Active Involvement in Learning

Adults learn best when they are actively participating in the learning rather than being passive recipients. People learn by doing. In training, this is usually done on the job. In the learning environment, the job must be simulated as closely as possible. Allow participants to practice the skills being taught. You want to minimize time spent in presenting content and maximize the time spent in practice and application through role plays, case studies, demonstration and practice, participant presentations, and so forth (Mitchell, 1998).

Self-Directed Learning

Adult learners are responsible for their own learning and are capable of self-direction. Although adults need some structure, they resist being told what to do. The facilitator must engage the learners in a process of inquiry and decision making and not just "give" information or knowledge "to" them. When introducing various instructional strategies, the facilitator must provide the purpose (links to their need to know) and the instructions, while giving them latitude to complete the activity.

Trial and Error

Making mistakes is another way adults learn. According to Mitchell (1998), success motivates adults and makes them want to learn more, but they tend to remember mistakes and want to learn about how to correct them. Facilitators must allow participants to try new things, to make mistakes, and to learn from them. A safe environment for trial and error must be created. Likewise, the facilitator must be sure the successes are reinforced and that the learners capture those lessons learned.

Building on Experience

Adults learn by connecting new information with what they already know (Mitchell, 1998). It is the building-block idea of moving from the known to the unknown. Because learning participants come with different backgrounds, the facilitator must discover what the participants know and build on that knowledge. Some techniques that can help the facilitator understand the audience's knowledge and experience base include: pretests; "icebreakers" (see chapter 4), an exercise or activity that brings everyone to a common understanding; participant profiles; and soliciting pre-course information by having participants respond to the course objectives.

Experience is a rich resource for adult learning. In any group of adults, there is a wide variety of backgrounds and experiences. The facilitator can leverage the different experiences for a richer learning experience through facilitative discussions, case studies, role plays, simulations, and the like.

The downside to experience is that the adult learner can also bring a set of biases, presuppositions, and bad habits that can inhibit learning. The facilitator must help learners examine these areas and replace or enhance them with new ideas, concepts, and perspectives.

Sensory Learning

Although adult learners use all their senses (sight, hearing, touch, smell, and taste), individuals usually have a dominant or preferred sense upon which they rely for learning new things (Mitchell, 1998). For all practical purposes, learning facilitation usually addresses the senses of sight (visual learning), hearing (auditory learning), and touch (kinesthetic learning).

Visual learners must interact with and apply content in a visual way. This means that as much as possible, they must see what they are learning. This need can be met in a variety of ways, from graphics to the printed page. Auditory learners must interact with and apply content through listening and speaking. This need must be met by providing auditory versions of content (from lecture to music) and by providing multiple opportunities for learners to hear and speak to each other. Kinesthetic learners must interact with and apply content in a physical way. Although the obvious way to meet this need is to provide hands-on practice, this need can also be met by providing ways for learners to interact with content physically (from note-taking to drawing pictures).

Effective facilitators "create a variety of sensory input because what isn't clear when received by one sense often crystallizes through another" (Mitchell, 1998). Additional information about learning preferences and styles appears in the next chapter.

Less Is More

Effective facilitators take complex or new material and organize it in a simple way for participants so they can easily understand and apply the new information and skills. So, why is it that some instructors and trainers feel a need to cram all the content they can into a course? As content experts, they want to give the learners all of their content. Yet, this very practice inhibits learning.

A large part of this issue relates to the initial design of the course. Content should directly align with specific learning objectives; other content should not be included, as was discussed in chapter 1. When you are handed such a design, it is clear what content is critical and how you should focus your facilitation. When your course design does not have this component, you can fall into a trap of trying to do it all in as little time as possible, which can cause you to lose focus and get off track. This causes you to eliminate the skill practices and present more content to save time, which ultimately causes learning to suffer.

Building on Theory

Theory is important to understanding—an important prerequisite to learning. Having participants understand why the learning is important and putting it in context makes the learning easier. However, this must be balanced with their orientation to learning; theory cannot simply be discussed in a vacuum.

Adults want theory presented in the context of the job and applicability to real-life situations. Facilitators need to explain the "what and why" of the course and any content within the course, and then make clear the course's relevance to the learners' situations. Before participating in a learning experience, adult learners want to know why they must learn the information. Once they buy into their need to know, they will invest significant energy in the learning experience.

The facilitator must be able to link the course objectives and content to the adult learners' need to know. The facilitator must demonstrate the value of the learning as it relates to the learners' personal or professional lives. A facilitator can tell them of the value, but it is better if the learners become aware of this through self-discovery of their gaps as they relate to the course content. Finally, debriefing activities should reinforce their need to know.

The facilitator should bring examples and applications to life by making them directly relevant to the learners' situations. Draw on personal life and work experience to make your examples real to the learners.

Practice

Orientation to learning is life- or work-centered for adults. Adults want to learn things that will help them solve a problem, do a task, or prepare for a position. Therefore, a key ingredient is practice, practice, practice. Practice not only increases proficiency, but also increases the probability of retention.

If you run short on time, practice is not where you want to cut corners. Practice is critical to learning and on-the-job application. Think of other ways (discussed in chapter 6) to make up time.

Feedback

Adults want and need feedback. People like and need to know how they are doing. As a facilitator, there are several ways you can provide feedback. A common way is testing. This should be for feedback and to identify areas that need additional work plus areas where there is adequate knowledge. You can also use checklists to provide feedback on practices, role plays, and case studies. Peer learners can provide feedback, and you can help facilitate this process. When discussing ideas as a group, you can clarify and provide feedback on participants' comments. When you debrief activities, provide feedback to your participants on the quality and completeness of their work. Summarize with lessons learned.

Individual Differences

Adult learners have individual differences. Every participant is unique and learns differently. Each brings different backgrounds, perspectives, and biases to the learning experience. As a facilitator, you need to recognize and positively respond to these differences.

Adults learn at their own pace. Not everyone is a fast learner. This variation can prove challenging for a facilitator. Ideally, you will have some knowledge of your audience prior to facilitating the course. If not, you can plan to address the needs of all, whether they are slow, regular, or fast learners. When you do that, you will focus on the largest group: the regular learners.

Your job is then to bring the slow learners along while challenging the fast learners. You may need to spend some extra time with slow learners or provide some remedial information. Fast learners can

- ▶ be given lead roles in your program
- ▶ provide peer coaching

Think About This

The acronym *LEARN*, suggested by an unknown but wise person, summarizes the principles of adult learning:

L earner-directed: Adult learners like to be in charge of their own learning as much as possible. Group or individual work in which they decide on structure, format, and application is effective. And, if adults understand why they need the information you can give them (which supports their self-direction), the content will be easier for them to learn.

E xperiential: Adults in a learning environment gain more from experiencing the concepts being taught than they do from just a lecture or presentation. They want active involvement and relevance to their job and organization. This involves practicing and applying the concepts rather than lecture only.

A ble to be evaluated: When teaching a concept, define it. Specify as clearly as possible the result wanted from the learners. Identify what knowledge, skill, or attitude change will take place. Focus facilitation on reaching that goal and measure it.

R esidual: Adults learn more effectively if they build on known information, facts, and/or experiences rather than from independent, arbitrary facts. Base the information provided on their experience and knowledge and lead them into more depth of that knowledge.

N umerous instructional methods: Some people learn better from verbal instructions, some from written instructions, and some from example. Others are visually oriented, and still others learn by trial and error. Incorporate various methods and types of activities into the program. You can reach a wider audience by using several instructional methods, plus variety provides valuable reinforcement and makes the course more interesting.

- ▶ serve as resources to others
- ▶ take on additional and more challenging tasks
- ▶ present some content
- ▶ lead group activities.

Individual differences become greater with age and experience. Some of these differences are learning styles, time and place of learning, and depth of knowledge and expertise. Facilitators cannot control all of these variables, but they can accommodate different learning styles and depth of knowledge. Alter learning activities to accommodate learning styles. Through the expertise of the facilitator and leveraging the expertise of the group, a facilitator can bring more depth and job relevance to the learning experience.

Getting It Done

In this chapter, you were introduced to the main differences between presenters and facilitators and the implications of those differences for learning experiences. You also learned about how adults learn and about facilitation techniques and strategies that support adult learners.

Exercise 2-1 provides you with an opportunity to identify which adult learning principles are most meaningful to you as a facilitator—and to plan how you will incorporate adult learning principles into your facilitation.

Exercise 2-1. Applying the principles of adult learning.

Listed below are principles of adult learning. Using the following scale, indicate the extent to which you believe and support these principles in your role as a facilitator of learning:

0 = not at all

1 = to a very little extent

2 = to some extent

3 = to a great extent

4 = to a very great extent.

Then, in the right-hand column, indicate how or what methods you will use to incorporate that principle in your facilitation on learning.

Principle	Rating					Methods
Learner readiness is critical to success.	0	1	2	3	4	
Adults learn best when they are actively participating in the learning rather than being passive recipients.	0	1	2	3	4	
Adult learners are responsible for their own learning and are capable of self-direction.	0	1	2	3	4	
Making mistakes is another way adults learn.	0	1	2	3	4	
Adults learn by associating new information with what they already know.	0	1	2	3	4	
Although adult learners use all their senses (sight, hearing, touch, smell, and taste), individuals usually have a dominant or preferred sense upon which they rely for learning new things.	0	1	2	3	4	
Less is more.	0	1	2	3	4	
Theory is important to understanding—an important prerequisite to learning—but it must be presented in the context of the job and applicability to real-life situations.	0	1	2	3	4	
Orientation to learning is life- or work-centered for adults; therefore, practice is critical.	0	1	2	3	4	
Adults want and need feedback.	0	1	2	3	4	
Adult learners have individual differences.	0	1	2	3	4	

Adapted from Mitchell, G. (1998). *The Trainer's Handbook: The AMA Guide to Effective Training,* 3d edition. New York: AMACOM.

In the next chapter, you will explore more deeply the two roles of learner and facilitator: For learners, you'll explore learning styles and preferences; and for facilitators, you'll learn more about competencies, multiple facilitator roles, and ways to assess facilitation quality.

3

Learner and Facilitator

■■

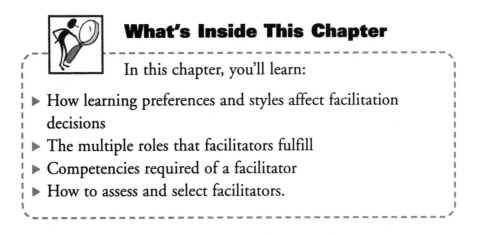

What's Inside This Chapter

In this chapter, you'll learn:

▶ How learning preferences and styles affect facilitation decisions
▶ The multiple roles that facilitators fulfill
▶ Competencies required of a facilitator
▶ How to assess and select facilitators.

The most important skill one can gain is the ability to learn. People need to understand their learning styles to maximize their learning effectiveness. Facilitators need an understanding of learning styles so they can incorporate them into the classroom experience.

Adults retain about 10 percent of what they read, 20 percent of what they hear, 30 percent of what they see, and 50 percent of what they hear and see. But, if adults become actively involved in their learning, those percentages rise to 70 percent of what they say and 90 percent of what they both say and do (Mitchell, 1998). Facilitators can achieve this high level of involvement and learning for participants by becoming an expert at a variety of instructional and facilitative methods—and tailoring them to the learning styles and needs of the learners.

Learning Preferences: How People Take In Information

In chapter 2 you were introduced to the three main learning preferences: visual, auditory, and kinesthetic. If facilitators do an excellent job of meeting the needs of their kinesthetic (hands-on), visual, and auditory learners, they can dramatically increase learning. Although varied learning preferences are always accommodated in a good course design, the facilitator can improve the chances of learning by also tailoring facilitation methods to the learning preferences of the specific group of participants.

Noted

Research has shown that about 36 percent of people are kinesthetic learners, 34 percent are auditory learners, and 29 percent are visual learners (Rose, 1987).

Visual Learning Preference

Visual learners take in and process information through what they see. They learn best from printed information, pictures, graphics, and the like. Incorporating some of the following in your delivery accommodates the visual learner's preferences:

▶ overhead transparencies
▶ flipcharts
▶ wallboards
▶ demonstrations
▶ diagrams, charts, and drawings
▶ participant materials such as manuals, reference material, prework reading assignments, and workbooks
▶ interactive computer simulations
▶ videos.

Auditory Learning Preference

Auditory learners take in and process information that is heard, including words, alliteration, and songs. To aid the learner with an auditory preference, you can incorporate

▶ presentations and lectures
▶ facilitative discussions
▶ demonstrations
▶ group projects and activities with feedback
▶ verbal instructions

- audiovisuals
- songs
- background instrumental music
- panel discussions
- question-and-answer sessions
- rhymes, chants, and poetry.

Kinesthetic Learning Preference

Kinesthetic, or physical, learners take in and process information through physical experiences. They like direct involvement and learning. The kinesthetic learning preference directly relates to hands-on training and skill building. Some things you can do include the following:

- hands-on practice
- role plays
- behavior modeling
- structured note taking (learners fill in blanks on handouts)
- simulations
- individual and group activities and projects
- having learners develop their own materials, such as drawings, flipcharts, and posters
- interactive computer simulations.

Noted

The next time you see a learner who is doodling on his or her materials, think twice before assuming that this learner is bored. Kinesthetic learners doodle during lectures and other activities that provide little or no physical experience. They help themselves physically interact with the content by doodling and thereby keep themselves engaged in the learning.

Learning Preferences and the Facilitator

The more adults see, hear, say, and do, the greater the learning and retention. Therefore, facilitators need to use a variety of instructional strategies and media to address learner preferences.

For example, although you still need to do some presenting, facilitated discussion allows others to voice their views and experiences (auditory learning preference). This approach also provides variety in presentation of content. Instructional strategies, such as simulations, group activities, demonstrations, practice, and role plays, provide learners with the opportunity to not only experience the content in a variety of ways, but also to meet the learning preferences of the participants. For the kinesthetic learner, it is important that lessons learned from these activities are reinforced and applied to job situations. When you use multiple forms of media, you meet the needs of the visual learner. When learners work and discuss together, you are providing an auditory experience. Your challenge is to incorporate as many of these options simultaneously in the facilitation of learning as possible.

Table 3-1 provides a way for you to select learning activities according to how participants take in information, that is, their learning preferences.

Basic Rule 3
Use multiple forms of media and learning strategies to support learners' taking in of content.

Learning Styles: How Adults Process Information

Now that you have an understanding of how learners take in information (learner preferences), you can move on to how learners process that information. The different ways that people process information are called learning styles, of which there are five: achievers, evaluators, networkers, socializers, and observers.

Achievers

Achievers focus on doing and accomplishing results and generally have the expertise to do so. People with this learning style are good at finding practical uses for ideas and theories. They enjoy being involved in new and challenging experiences and carrying out plans to meet those challenges. Achievers have the ability to solve problems, make decisions, and develop action plans based on implementing solutions to question or problems. They want to find practical uses for the ideas and training content. Achievers like to accept the lead role in addressing those challenges.

Table 3-1. Aligning learning activities and media with learning preferences.

Kinesthetic	Auditory	Visual
Supervised practice on the job	Lectures	Diagrams
Simulations	Discussions	Charts and graphs
Paper-and-pencil tests	Demonstrations	Graphics
Physical analogies	Brainstorming	Color
Note taking	Question-and-answer sessions	Training manuals
Flowcharting	Songs and lyrics	Reading
Case histories	Music	Handouts
Group projects	Coaching	Flowcharts
Role playing	Rhymes	Flipcharts
Physical demonstrations	Acronyms	Wallboards/posters
Hands-on activities	Metaphors	Whiteboards
Building things	Definitions	Reference materials
Puzzles	Small group work	Lists of parts or definitions
Charades	Panel discussions	Films/videos
Writing on flipcharts or wallboards	Group or individual presentations	Slides
Whiteboards	Group projects	Maps
Tools	Films	Observation
Props	Audiovisuals	Demonstrations
Toys	"War stories"	Posters and art
Job aids	Interactive computer simulations	Slides and photos
Interactive computer simulations		PowerPoint presentations
		Interactive computer simulations

Reprinted with permission from Performance Advantage Group, 2003.

Achievers like sequence and logical order and clear, step-by-step directions. Achievers are not strong in people orientation and have a tendency to take control with little regard for others' feelings.

Because achievers are "take charge" people, you may need to rotate small group leadership roles to give other learners a chance. For achievers, the facilitator needs to be practical and present what will really work back on the job. Facilitate the application-to-the-job material, ensuring completion of the activity. Be sure to allow learners to present their work so participants can learn from others. You may consider beginning the session with a review of a performance contract if one was used (see chapter 5) to start achievers thinking about the application of the course content. Revisit the performance contract often.

Think About This

To accommodate the learning style of achievers, you, as facilitator, can incorporate case studies, role plays, and action learning and then debrief them emphasizing the real-world situations. Allow adequate time for the development of action plans for on-the-job application of the new knowledge, skills, and abilities (KSAs). Facilitative discussions and presentations should emphasize the link to the job in real-world terms. For example, you can ask, "How would you do this differently next time?"

In small group work the achiever may monopolize the conversation, dictate the direction and solution, and show little respect or patience for others' opinions or experience. They want the activity's directions stated logically in writing with specific outcomes identified. You may need to revisit course ground rules concerning everyone's participation, the values of others' opinions, and mutual respect.

Evaluators

Sometimes referred to as thinkers, evaluators like to analyze a situation and use a logical process to resolve issues. They ask many detailed questions and in so doing collect a great deal of information. They are very concerned about working within the existing guidelines. Evaluators are good at assimilating a wide range of information and putting it into concise, logical form, like lists, charts, or planning tools. These learners are more interested in the basis of theory and application of theory and less on building relationships. The theory you present needs to be logically sound, exact, and supported by facts.

Evaluators need to see value and job-relatedness of learning activities and the course content, for that matter. They want to set up an orderly way (logical steps) to address the purpose of the activity. Be aware, though, that the evaluator may challenge the expertise of the achiever and others.

Networkers

These learners like to develop close relationships with others and avoid interpersonal conflict. Because they are good listeners, they develop strong people networks. They are more compliant than others and are often easily swayed. Networkers try to avoid

Think About This

To accommodate the learning style of evaluators, be sure to provide a summary of the theoretical basis of the content. Your debriefing of activities could take the form of building on the results and then going into application to the job. Depending on the training design, you can also facilitate case studies, individual projects, and reading or research. In a group activity, the evaluator will want to know in detail the instructions, outcome, format of their presentation, sources of information, and ways to access that information.

risks, seek consensus, and are slower than others to make decision. In group activities, networkers rarely disagree with others' opinions, but rather are supportive of others and seek collaboration. Networkers take time to build trust and get personally acquainted with others. Although they are outgoing, they need direct feedback as a way of support.

Think About This

You can use networkers to stimulate group interaction and involvement. Ask them what they think of others' ideas. Provide direct feedback to their comments and contributions to group projects. Allow networkers to take the lead in ice-breaking activities. Provide networkers opportunities for interaction in small groups and one-on-one activities. They respond well to peer teaching and tutoring.

Socializers

These learners like to talk and share. They like the spotlight and like to have fun. Although they like to get multiple perspectives, they are good at selling their ideas to others and building alliances. Socializers are not concerned with details or facts. They like to keep a fast pace and make quick, spontaneous decisions. In group work, the socializer wants to work quickly, seek others' input, persuade others, get it done quickly, provide some humor, and volunteer to make the presentation.

Think About This

When you are a facilitator, you can use the socializer's outgoing nature to stimulate group interaction. Socializers may be frustrated if the program goes too slowly for them. You may need to indicate for their benefit that not all learners are as fast as they are when it comes to learning new ideas and skills. When providing instruction for learning activities, remind them that the process of arriving at decisions is as important as the decisions themselves.

Socializers like presentations of group activities and must be reminded that a presentation requires depth; superficial responses are not enough. To accomplish this, ask socializers for their rationale or for the facts behind their comments. Strive to take them deeper into the content. In large group discussions, recognize their contributions but ask for alternative views. Socializers are good at brainstorming activities.

Observers

These learners are best at viewing concrete situations from many different points of view. They prefer to observe and conceptualize rather than take action. They are reflective thinkers. They enjoy situations that call for generating not just many ideas, but also a wide range of ideas. These learners are more interested in abstract ideas and concepts and less in building relationships. Observers want to take time to reflect and conceptualize and don't like to wing it.

You'll want to create an experience, involve observers in that experience, and let them reflect on it. Debriefing of activities could take the form of building on the results and going into more abstract ideas, such as generating future situations. Depending on the training design, you can also facilitate case studies and follow-up with "what if" scenarios to allow for changing conditions.

Basic Rule 4

Use multiple forms of media and learning strategies to support different learning styles.

Think About This

You'll find when you facilitate group learning that demonstrations, case studies, and brainstorming are good ways to meet the needs of observers, especially if they have had the opportunity for individual work first. These activities can be followed up with "what if" scenarios. You can also ask open-ended questions and flipchart the responses. You'll want them to present their process for solving a case and the lessons learned, which link back to the course content. As a facilitator, you will want to provide time for participants to reflect on what they have experienced and make some notes about the meaning of those experiences and their application to the participants' job or situation.

Who's What Kind of Learner?

As a facilitator, you will want to recognize the five different learning styles and address all the learners' needs. A quick way to tentatively identify these styles is through the learners' choices of words and behaviors. Table 3-2 provides a brief summary of verbal cues and learner behavior to help you recognize these styles.

Now that you know about learner preferences for taking in content and learner styles for processing content, you, as a facilitator, will want to use both sets of information in making a conscious decision regarding meeting the needs of your learners. Table 3-3 integrates learning preferences and styles with your learning activity choices.

Roles of a Facilitator

Facilitators wear many hats during the course of a learning event, and all these hats are critical to supporting an effective learning experience. An apt analogy might be director of a play or movie: The director orchestrates everything that happens, from what the actors say and do down to minute details of set design. These elements interact to support the goal of telling a story.

By the same token, all the roles facilitators fill and all the things facilitators do interact to support one goal: learning. While wearing these many hats, facilitators are also in charge of both the task (learning and applying knowledge and skills) and the process (how the learning and applying happen) of learning experiences. Each role described in the sections that follow focuses on managing a task or process.

Basic Rule 5

Facilitate both the task and process of learning experiences.

Table 3-2. Recognizing learning styles.

Role	Verbal Cue	Learner Behavior
Achiever	Tells, does little asking Blunt, to the point Asks for clear directions Asks for clear, concise answers Asks for application to the job	Does lots of talking Takes charge, likes to be leader Follows the participant guide, in order Demonstrates little patience for non-task-related activities
Evaluator	Asks for data, facts, sources Focused comments on the topic Little personal sharing Wants the details	Task oriented Follows directions Challenges others' expertise Develops steps to accomplish activities
Networker	Asks many questions Does little telling Vocalizes support for others' opinions Seeks attention and feedback	Engages in effective listening Seeks collaboration and consensus Reserves personal opinions Avoids conflict Develops close relationships Builds trust
Socializer	Shares experiences Tells stories Digresses and gets off the subject Readily expresses personal opinion Talks a lot Uses language of persuasion	Makes quick, spontaneous decisions without all the information Gets multiple perspectives Has fun Loves group activities and discussions
Observer	Likes to conceptualize, "what if" discussions Asks questions or makes comments off the direct subject Makes "what about this" statements Makes future application to discussions	Provides several alternatives to a problem or situation Easily gets off the subject Wants fuller discussion on the idea Not concerned with the concrete application of the ideas

Reprinted with permission from Performance Advantage Group, 2003.

Table 3-3. Aligning activities with learning preferences and styles.

Learning Activity	Visual Preference	Auditory Preference	Kinesthetic Preference	Achiever Style	Evaluator Style	Networker Style	Socializer Style	Observer Style
Lecture		X		X	X			
Handouts	X			X	X			X
Group Discussion		X				X	X	X
Role Play			X	X	X		X	X[1]
Group Work at Flipchart	X	X	X			X	X	X
Case Study		X		X	X			X
Hands-on Practice			X	X				
Note Taking	X		X		X			X
Games	X	X	X	X		X	X	
Small Group Work		X		X[2]		X	X	X[3]
Activity Debriefing		X		X	X			X
Action Planning			X	X	X			X
Brainstorming		X		X		X	X	

[1] If they observe and don't participate in the action
[2] If they have a leadership role
[3] If opportunity is given to comment on observations during activity

Reprinted with permission from Deb Tobey LLC, 2003.

Leader of the Group

Everything you say and do focuses on helping participants learn. As leader, you create and sustain the environment so that interaction with you and other participants motivates them to acquire new knowledge and skills that you and others possess. Your role is to help participants learn and apply the new knowledge and skills to their jobs.

In this leader role, the facilitator is in charge of leading both the task and the process aspects of learning. In the process area, facilitators:

- ▶ lead how the group of learners interacts
- ▶ support the learning of the group
- ▶ help learners apply the new knowledge and skills to their jobs.

A facilitator encourages group cohesiveness and direction throughout the participation process. The facilitator must manage the group involvement process, ensuring group members are treated as equals, encouraging group discussion, suggesting decision-making and problem-solving alternatives, guiding toward resolution, and promoting development of actions and follow-up plans. As leader, the facilitator must help team members to be sensitive to other members, involve all members, and establish and maintain group norms to help them function more effectively.

One of the things leaders do in leading the task component is provide feedback on participants' comments and individual and group activities. Individual comments and group discussions are ideal times to assess if the learners are really getting it. Your response gives them additional content and, at the same time, feedback on their understanding of the subject under discussion. Practice activities are great opportunities to provide balanced feedback.

Basic Rule 6
As leader, you help participants learn and apply the new knowledge and skills to their jobs.

Manager of the Agenda

Having developed a schedule, it is your job to maintain that agenda; this is a task-focused facilitator role. Starting on time, whether in the morning or after breaks, can be difficult to enforce. Even when starting on time is a ground rule, it is difficult to

Noted

Many times, facilitators are tempted to give only positive feedback by affirming what a learner has said, rather than correcting or augmenting it. Some facilitators agree with people's comments, even if they are incomplete or wrong. This is a disservice to all concerned. Although affirmation is important (and, if nothing else, the learner's effort and participation can always be affirmed), giving complete and honest feedback is also important. A facilitator cannot allow his or her duty to provide balanced feedback to be affected by a participant's intimidating job title, or a need to be liked and respected (more on facilitators' personal agendas later). Simply put, the facilitator owes the group and the individual correct and complete feedback on all practice activities.

manage to that agreed-upon rule. Yet, starting on time and staying on time are important to completing all the content and fully experiencing the learning strategies.

Once you get behind, you must make up time without sacrificing the quality of the learning experience. The learners will notice if you take longer than the schedule states for an activity. Some will worry that the learning is compromised, and others will be so busy making sure you take a break at the right time that they will miss the learning!

You must also manage the time for facilitative discussion and for various learning activities. It is very easy to respond to a question and then go down the garden path of various topics. Related? Yes. Important to meeting the objectives of the course? Well, maybe.

Think About This

Should you share your course time schedule with the learners? Except for telling them what time breaks, meals, and the end of the day are, the answer is most often no. If you are facilitating properly, you are constantly adjusting to the needs of the learners within the timeframes that you have. If you share actual agenda item times with them, they will be more interested in whether you are keeping to the schedule than in the learning.

Learning activities pose another opportunity to challenge your skills. All groups are different. With best intentions, you begin the activity according to schedule. With clear instructions, the groups begin their work. Then as the time draws near, they need just a few more minutes. Their presentations take longer than expected. The debriefing session draws questions. You are now off schedule.

With all these possibilities for getting off schedule, you are still expected to finish on time. After all, this is a ground rule. Although you may be able to negotiate some extra time at the end of the day or have a working lunch, there is still the expectation of stopping on time. After all, you're the leader and you manage the agenda.

Basic Rule 7
Manage and maintain your agenda.

Role Model for Positive Behaviors

You must always—without exception—maintain a positive and professional demeanor; this is a critical part of your focus on process. While it can be tough, seek positive solutions to constructive conflict; try to see the other's point of view. Your modeling of professional behavior is critical to having a successful program.

Beyond this, model the behavior that you are teaching. For example, if you are teaching coaching skills, model the behavior of an exemplary coach. When explaining concepts, providing feedback, or making application to the job, model those coaching behaviors you are teaching. By so doing, participants can learn by observing and become more convinced that these skills really do work.

Basic Rule 8
Always maintain a positive and professional demeanor and model the behavior that you are teaching.

Content Expert

Being an expert in your content is part of your task. To some extent, facilitators have credibility by virtue of standing before the group, and you will not want to lose that credibility. The participants expect you to be a content expert, someone who's able to speak beyond the script of the leader's guide and make the content relevant to them.

How do you do this? One way is to ask and answer questions. You ask questions that take people deeper into the content than they currently are. By then taking their answers and going further or making application, you demonstrate your grasp of the content. You can have the same impact by answering questions completely, when appropriate. The familiar technique of handing it back to the group ("What do you think about that?") can only work for so long. At some point, participants want to know what you think and why. This is an opportunity for you to enhance your stance as a content expert.

Besides asking and answering questions, you can also share your experiences—not all experiences, but those relevant to the course content and application of that content to the job. As a content expert, you can blend your knowledge and your job-related experience to enrich the learning experience. Your stories can make the content come alive, capture the interest of the group, and enhance your credibility as a content expert and facilitator. These things do not just happen. As you prepare to facilitate, plan for your questions and ways of sharing your experiences. If you just ad lib, you're likely to stray from the learning objectives and lose your learners along the way.

Jargon is also important for the content expert. You must know and speak the language of your participants. There is nothing more embarrassing than having a participant ask a question and you not having a clue as to what he or she is saying. Your command of the language of the subject will go a long way to establishing and maintaining your credibility.

Basic Rule 9

Demonstrate mastery of the subject, in both content and application to the job.

Consultant

In your role of a consultant or advisor or coach, you are to help the participants complete a critical task: to make sense of the concepts and apply them to their jobs within the context of their environment. This is the task part of learning, which goes beyond having learners complete action plans or a performance contract. You must help them see the implications of new knowledge and skills for their performance, that of their team, and that of their business unit (process of learning). After all, the ultimate purpose of your course is to close an identified performance gap that is important to the individual and the organization.

Your consultant role may take you beyond the classroom. In some cases (within reason), you may need to do some one-on-one consulting with persons during lunch, break, or even during the evening. Yes, you must do your preparation work for the next day and, yes, you must meet the needs of your participants. You may even have the opportunity to do some follow-up work to see the extent that the new knowledge and skills have transferred to the job. In your role as a consultant, you go beyond the classroom into the work environment. You can then identify enablers and barriers to knowledge and skill transfer, and help management address the situation. Ultimately, you are a business problem solver.

Basic Rule 10
Consult with learners to clarify content and help them apply the content to their jobs, within their environment.

Facilitator Competencies

When most people talk of competencies, they usually think of knowledge and skills. In a broader sense, however, competencies also include individual characteristics (for example, supportiveness, achievement orientation, initiative), which are manifested as behaviors. Facilitator characteristics drive facilitator behaviors, which then drive the facilitator's job performance—the facilitation of learning. Figure 3-1 illustrates this domino effect.

With this as a background, let's look at some competencies that facilitators should possess. For ease of understanding, the competencies are grouped by major categories accompanied by behavioral descriptions that align with that category.

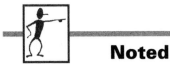

Noted

Additional factors external to the facilitator can affect performance as well. However, these factors—including recognition and rewards, culture, and organization climate—are beyond the scope of this book.

Knowledge competencies for a facilitator include the knowledge of the following:

- ▶ the organization: its strategies, objectives, markets, customers, competitors, products/services, and so on
- ▶ adult learning principles
- ▶ learning theory and how it is applied to learning
- ▶ training evaluation
- ▶ needs assessment for the specific seminar or workshop to be facilitated
- ▶ organizational, job, and individual performance indicators
- ▶ instructional design and development
- ▶ diversity awareness as it relates to the implications of participant differences on learning
- ▶ methods and tactics to get organizational buy-in and support for learning
- ▶ group dynamics
- ▶ tactics for coaching and feedback.

Figure 3-1. Individual characteristics drive performance.

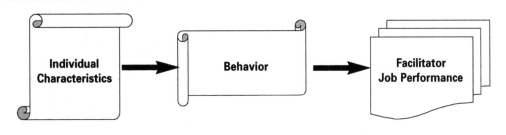

Skill competencies for learning facilitators include:

- ▶ operating equipment: overhead projectors, computers and LCD projectors, participant voting systems, and so forth
- ▶ writing on flipcharts: preparing standard charts and recording participants' comments
- ▶ communicating verbally to present information
- ▶ communicating nonverbally: body positioning, gestures, facial expressions
- ▶ summarizing and paraphrasing participant input
- ▶ providing coaching and feedback
- ▶ listening actively and effectively
- ▶ planning learning activities
- ▶ thinking in terms of systems to see interrelationships among participants' input by recognizing the connecting patterns.

Individual characteristics are best described as behavioral competencies. People demonstrate individual characteristics by how they behave in given situations. Table 3-4 is an extensive listing of these behavioral competencies, including a brief descriptor of each competency. There are 14 characteristic categories, each containing multiple behaviors.

For those not possessing a desired competency or if the competency is not yet a strength, training can help. The knowledge and skill competencies are relatively easy to learn. Although behavioral competencies are more difficult and take longer to develop, growth in this area is also possible. The more competencies a facilitator possesses and the more effectively he or she uses those competencies, the better the performance, which directly affects the quality of the learning experience.

Facilitator Selection

As you can see, there is a lot to being a good facilitator. It is so much more than just knowing the content or being able to present. To really make learning happen takes genuine skill. That point raises the question of how organizations select facilitators to guide the learning. You may be in a situation where you must select facilitators from within your organization or from a vendor organization. What factors should you look at?

Table 3-4. Facilitator behavioral competencies.

The following table is a listing and description of facilitator characteristic groupings and behavioral competencies necessary for facilitating an organization classroom learning experience. The total behavior competency model for a facilitator (inside and outside the classroom) is more extensive.

Characteristic Grouping	Behavioral Competencies
Initiative	1. Positions the learning experience with participants by building relationships and setting the climate 2. Positions the learning with participants to support the organization's strategies and objectives 3. Makes extra efforts to ensure participant learning and use of that learning on the job by focusing questions, examples, and plans on real-world examples 4. Takes self-directed action to remove learning and transfer barriers in order to effectively and efficiently achieve learning outcomes
Concern for Continuous Improvement	1. Utilizes adult learning principles to ensure learning 2. Monitors ongoing participant learning by soliciting feedback and analyzing performance on assessments 3. Plans and monitors facilitation to ensure efficient and effective use of time and greatest impact on learning
Customer Service	1. Acts as a learning consultant to participants 2. Implements instructional strategies relative to participant needs 3. Builds networks among participants to support classroom learning and transfer to the job
Interpersonal Understanding	1. Demonstrates and acts on an understanding of the collective concerns of the participants 2. Demonstrates and acts on an understanding of participants' personal interests, concerns, and motivations 3. Seeks to understand the motivations of participants' behavior
Leading Others	1. Promotes a spirit of cooperation among participants 2. Clarifies and communicates roles and expectations of facilitator and participants 3. Solicits the input of participants and leverages participant expertise through establishing collaborative relationships 4. Creates learner synergy through involvement in course instructional strategies 5. Recognizes and rewards the contribution of participants

(continued on page 42)

41

Table 3-4. Facilitator behavioral competencies (continued).

Characteristic Grouping	Behavioral Competencies
Developing Others	1. Creates a learning environment that fosters learning and transfer 2. Identifies job-related applications to course content 3. Contributes to individual, team, and corporate knowledge 4. Models development to support continuous learning 5. Provides coaching to enhance learning
Analytical/Problem Solving	1. Implements a structured process of collecting course information and feedback 2. Gathers the relevant information and takes action to resolve a problem or issue within the learning experience
Creativity and Innovation	1. Uncovers opportunities for application of learning 2. Takes innovative action to maximize the effectiveness of a learning experience 3. Implements creative instructional strategies
Change Management	1. Proactively recognizes situations where change in classroom learning is needed and initiates appropriate action 2. Redirects efforts and/or adapts approach in the face of changing course/participant requirements 3. Changes plans and acts in response to changing conditions or participant needs, rather than pursuing a single course of action 4. Ensures that the participants embrace the need for the new KSAs taught in the learning experience
Risk Taking	1. Takes appropriate risks to see new ideas, content, and instructional strategies accepted and/or implemented 2. Supports participants who take appropriate risks
Communicating Effectively	1. Makes effective verbal presentations (includes changing language or terminology to fit audience characteristics) 2. Reads and understands verbal and nonverbal behavior and responds appropriately 3. Effectively uses nonverbal communication techniques

Characteristic Grouping	Behavioral Competencies
Influencing	1. Facilitates in such a way as to influence the participants to accept and use the new KSAs 2. Uses interpersonal and communication skills to gain acceptance of and commitment to course content and learning objectives 3. Gains commitment of participants by positioning the learning in terms of benefits meaningful to the participants 4. Builds trust between facilitator and participants and among participants 5. Gains the cooperation and support of the participants
Organizational Awareness	1. Expresses the benefits and disadvantages of participants' input using their business terminology 2. Acts as a catalyst for participants and their respective business units to improve performance through the use of the acquired KSAs 3. Recognizes and responds to organizational issues as they relate to the course content 4. Thinks organizationally and presents learning applications that address participants' jobs and organizational needs 5. Demonstrates an understanding of the organization's strategies, objectives, markets, products/services, informal political network, and so forth
Personal Effectiveness Characteristics	1. Represents accurately and completely the training organization to participants 2. Serves as a role model for others regarding appropriate business conduct and ethical principles 3. Keeps emotions under control when facing adversity 4. Interacts effectively with varying levels of participants with different backgrounds and perspectives

Reprinted with permission from Performance Advantage Group, 2003.

First, you may need to do some research. You want facilitators who are content experts but who are also credible to your audience. Not all subject matter experts (SMEs) have the same credibility with your target audience. So, ask a few questions of potential learners about facilitator candidates and get a feel for what facilitator credibility means to them. For some learners, it's experience; for others, it's education; and for still others, it's something else.

Next, if you have the opportunity, you want to see the potential facilitators in action. You want to observe how they develop the learning environment, their communication and presentation/facilitation skills, how well they implement various learning activities, and how proficient they are in the use of media.

Sometimes you'll need to use someone from outside, perhaps a contractor/consultant or someone from a vendor organization. When you use someone who is an external source, you must add to your assessment items such questions as:

- Is there compatibility of cultures?
- Will the facilitator candidates abide by your code of ethics and policies?
- Can they meet your delivery schedule?
- Can they demonstrate success within your industry and with your type of audience?
- Are the facilitators dedicated to your organization?
- Will they sign a nondisclosure agreement?
- Is it a cost-effective solution?
- Do the facilitators have subject matter expertise?
- Will they be credible to your audience?
- Do they know your organization and can they make linkages of the content to your organization?
- Are they skilled facilitators?

Principles Underlying Facilitation of Learning

Professional, ethical, learner-centered, expert facilitation is critical to learners, organizations, and facilitators. The following principles are presented for your consideration. You are invited to make them your own.

1. Facilitated learning is learner-centered, not facilitator-centered.
2. The facilitator is in the learning experience with the learners; he or she is not merely an observer.

3. The facilitator's goal is to make learning happen.

4. Learners get first crack at the learning as much as possible.

5. Adult learners have specific needs that facilitators must fulfill for learning to occur.

6. Facilitators create opportunities for learners to share their own experiences and expertise.

7. In a learning event, all participants are sources for learning; the facilitator is not the only source of expertise.

8. Facilitators protect and affirm ideas.

9. Facilitators are not performers. The facilitator's job is to be interested, not interesting.

10. Facilitators encourage and support balanced participation in the learning group.

11. Facilitators create a comfortable and supportive environment in which learners can take risks.

12. Facilitators remove obstacles from the learning process.

Getting It Done

In this chapter, you learned a great deal about what it takes to be a facilitator. Exercise 3-1 will support your growth and development by allowing you to assess yourself in relation to facilitator roles.

Exercise 3-2 is a facilitation/presentation assessment tool that can be given to an observer who can augment your judgment about your competencies. To use the facilitation/presentation assessment tool, you are to:

1. Assign a weight to each behavior, totaling 100 points. Weights should reflect how each set of behaviors is valued by your organization.

2. Select a skilled facilitator and have that person assess your skills, using the assessment tool.

3. Use this feedback to develop areas rated 2 or below.

Compare these results with the results of your self-assessment. After you and the observer have completed the assessments, you'll have a roadmap for your development.

Exercise 3-1. Self-assessment role inventory.

This self-assessment is intended to help you reflect on your effectiveness regarding the various roles of a facilitator. Below are statements regarding the facilitator's roles. Using the scale provided, indicate the extent to which you fulfill that dimension of a particular role. For areas rated 2 or below, identify specific actions you will take to improve yourself in that area.

0 = not at all
1 = to a very little extent
2 = to a little or some extent
3 = to a great extent
4 = to a very great extent

Role	Rating					Actions
Leader of the Group						
Creates and sustains an environment conducive for learning	0	1	2	3	4	
Helps learners apply the content to their jobs	0	1	2	3	4	
Provides complete feedback during facilitative discussions	0	1	2	3	4	
Provides complete feedback following learning and practice activities	0	1	2	3	4	
Develops group cohesiveness	0	1	2	3	4	
Manages group involvement processes	0	1	2	3	4	
Promotes the development of action and follow-up plans	0	1	2	3	4	
Manager of the Agenda						
Establishes timing as a ground rule	0	1	2	3	4	
Starts sessions on time	0	1	2	3	4	
Manages the time to ensure content is covered	0	1	2	3	4	
Manages the time to ensure learning strategies are included	0	1	2	3	4	
Stops on time	0	1	2	3	4	

Role	Rating					Actions
Content Expert						
Asks in-depth questions	0	1	2	3	4	
Answers questions in depth and detail	0	1	2	3	4	
Shares experiences that enhance credibility	0	1	2	3	4	
Uses appropriate jargon for the topic and audience	0	1	2	3	4	
Role Model						
Maintains positive, professional demeanor	0	1	2	3	4	
Models behaviors being taught	0	1	2	3	4	
Consultant						
Helps participants understand the concepts	0	1	2	3	4	
Helps participants apply the concepts to their jobs	0	1	2	3	4	
Meets one-on-one with participants during the program	0	1	2	3	4	
Follows up with participants after the program to see if KSAs are being used on the job	0	1	2	3	4	
Identifies environmental factors that support the transfer of KSAs to the job	0	1	2	3	4	
Identifies environmental factors that hinder the transfer of KSAs to the job	0	1	2	3	4	
Addresses identified environmental factors that may support or inhibit job application	0	1	2	3	4	

Reprinted with permission from Performance Advantage Group, 2003.

Exercise 3-2. Facilitation/presentation assessment.

Below is a list of behaviors describing the demonstration of facilitation/presentation skills. As an assessor, assign a weight to each behavior, with the total being 100. Weights should reflect how each behavior is valued by your organization.

Then use the following scale to indicate the extent to which the individual demonstrates the listed behaviors.

0 = not at all
1 = to very little extent
2 = to a moderate extent
3 = to a great extent
4 = to a very great extent

Behavior	Weight	Rating				
Credibility						
1. Demonstrates appropriate personal and professional behavior		0	1	2	3	4
2. Demonstrates content knowledge (depth and breadth)		0	1	2	3	4
3. Makes linkages to organizational realities		0	1	2	3	4
Learning Environment						
4. Involves participants in establishing and maintaining the learning environment		0	1	2	3	4
5. Uses opening (warm-up) activities to gain participant involvement		0	1	2	3	4
6. Manages group interaction, draws in quiet participants, and manages participants who try to monopolize the interaction		0	1	2	3	4
7. Integrates adult learning principles into the course delivery		0	1	2	3	4
Communication Skills						
8. Uses appropriate verbal and nonverbal communication techniques		0	1	2	3	4
9. Uses examples that are familiar to the participants		0	1	2	3	4
10. Provides complete and timely feedback to participants		0	1	2	3	4
11. Provides time for participants to structure or frame questions, ask questions, and voice concerns and issues		0	1	2	3	4

Behavior	Weight	Rating				
Presentation/Facilitation Skills						
12. Effectively uses voice (tone, projection, inflection), gestures, and eye contact		0	1	2	3	4
13. Effectively uses examples, personal experiences, stories, and humor		0	1	2	3	4
14. Effectively uses various questioning techniques		0	1	2	3	4
15. Effectively paraphrases/restates participants' questions, comments, and observations		0	1	2	3	4
16. Promotes participant discussion and involvement		0	1	2	3	4
17. Keeps discussion on topic and activities focused on outcomes		0	1	2	3	4
Instructional/Learning Strategies						
18. Implements a variety of instructional/learning strategies (such as guided discussions, case studies, role plays, small group work with feedback, assessments)		0	1	2	3	4
19. Plans and facilitates debriefing sessions so all learning is processed		0	1	2	3	4
20. Adjusts activities, time, pace, content, and sequencing to accommodate specific learner needs		0	1	2	3	4
Media						
21. Uses media (video, overheads, computer projection, wallboards, props, flipcharts) effectively		0	1	2	3	4
22. Demonstrates ability to substitute, change, or add media as needed		0	1	2	3	4
	100					

Upon completion, multiply the weight of each behavior by the rating and add up the total column. The total will be between 0 and 400. This is the participant's assessment score. The score for passing (determined by the individual's organization) is _____. Develop actions to improve areas rated 2 or below.

Reprinted with permission from Performance Advantage Group, 2003.

This chapter introduced you to the multiple roles and expectations of a facilitator, and discussed the implications of learner preferences and styles for those roles. In the next chapter, you will focus on the elements that come together to ensure the best start for a learning event.

4

Getting Started

▪ ▪

What's Inside This Chapter

In this chapter, you'll learn about creating the climate for learning by:

▶ Getting to know your audience prior to learning and as learning begins
▶ Paying attention to room setup and the physical environment
▶ Using your own behavior and style
▶ Using effective opening activities to set the tone
▶ Personalizing your facilitation.

Getting started on the right foot for a learning event can make a huge difference in how much learning takes place throughout your course. You need to put the learners at ease, learn about them, set the expectation for participation and involvement, and ultimately create a climate that supports and enhances learning.

Know Your Audience

In an ideal situation, you have all the information you need about your audience before you begin facilitating your course so that you can begin tailoring your facilitation to the needs of the specific learners. The course designer's or leader's guide should provide you with the following information about the learners:

> ▶ skill and background levels relevant to the content you will be facilitating, and the mix you will have of experienced and not-so-experienced learners

> ▶ job context information, including whether the participants work alone or in groups; levels of activity and movement that they are accustomed to; and where they are in their work cycle when they come to you (for example, if they will just be ending the graveyard shift and coming to your class exhausted)

> ▶ learning styles and preferences and types of learning activities that they are accustomed to (and not accustomed to!)

> ▶ flexibility, openness to change, willingness to try new learning modes and ways of doing things

> ▶ expectations the learners have for the course and attitudes they have toward the subject and the learning event

> ▶ circumstances under which they are present at the learning event (for example, if it's a mandatory course, or if they need to improve job performance or prepare for impending changes).

If you don't have this information and you have time prior to the learning event to collect it, you can interview, survey, or conduct a focus group with a sample of the learners. Alternatively you may speak with the learners' supervisors or with other facilitators who have worked with these learners. There may be evaluation data from other courses these learners have participated in that you can consult, or

Basic Rule 11

Know as much as you can about your learner audience.

organizational data might be available regarding the learners (performance reports, quality reports, employee attitude surveys, and so forth).

If you don't have this information prior to the course opening, and you don't have time prior to the learning event to collect the information, you have two options. You can prepare a couple of contingency activities based on what you deduce to be some of the most likely information. Alternatively, you can develop an opening activity that will allow you to gather some of the information.

Think About This

What kinds of opening activities can help you gather learner information? Try spending a few moments asking targeted questions of the early-arriving learners or handing out a short, written survey to learners as they enter the room. You could also conduct a small group activity in which learners share their expectations for the learning event, questions, concerns about the subject matter, or anecdotes that illustrate their experience and background with the subject matter.

Creating the Climate for Learning

Critical aspects of creating a climate for learning include setting up the room and adjusting physical environment factors before the learning event; preparing yourself for the facilitation experience; greeting the learners as they arrive; making the learners feel comfortable as they arrive; and conducting opening activities.

Think About This

One factor that will affect all your decisions about creating a climate for learning is the number of learners who will be participating in the event. Facilitated learning rarely involves more than 24 learners. Therefore, you probably won't need—or want—a huge room or a large number of tables and chairs for learners. In addition, it is unlikely that you'd need a microphone to amplify your voice, although there may be some occasions when you'd want to use a lavaliere microphone, which would allow you to move freely throughout the room.

Room Setup and Seating Arrangements

How a room is set up is an important part of creating the learning climate and can be an important factor in enhancing—or hindering—the learning. Because of this, you will want to give thought as to how your room is set before you begin facilitating a learning event. Of course, in some cases there are limits as to how much you can do to set or reset a room. Some examples will help clarify these limits:

▶ *Example 1:* You're taking a workshop on the road and delivering it in hotels. The hotel indicates that the room will hold up to 30. Because you only expect 16–20 participants, there should be plenty of room, right? Not necessarily! Many hotels determine the room capacity by lecture style. You can get many more people in a room set lecture style than you can in rounds or a U-shaped setup. Also, the capacity does not tell you the room's dimensions. Many hotel rooms are rectangular and narrow with columns. Again, this configuration is not ideal for a learning room setup.

▶ *Example 2:* You're taking the workshop to another company location. They have a training room with the media requirements and the right size. They tell you that they use the room for training. You later realize that it is computer skills training or another type that has fixed desks, usually lecture style. Again, this limits your capability to do small group work and lead facilitative discussion.

▶ *Example 3:* In many cases, you want breakout rooms for group activities. You must make sure that the rooms have the necessary supplies. If you indicate that you need breakout rooms for small group work that requires charting and you get whiteboards, there is a problem. Participants cannot take the whiteboard to the main room for read-outs. Can they copy it over? Yes, but this takes additional time and then others cannot see their work. In addition, many times breakout rooms are on different floors or spread out, limiting your ability to monitor and coach the various groups.

▶ *Example 4:* Some locations have an executive boardroom or meeting room. In some cases, these rooms are auditorium and pit style. Such rooms are good for making presentations, but they are not good for facilitating learning. The image of meeting in the executive room is nice, but the learning will suffer.

Basic Rule 12
Find out the true usability of a room before delivery.

So, what's the point of these examples? You must do a little research and be sure the room is appropriate for the type of learning experience you are facilitating. If it is not appropriate, do all you can to change rooms, and be very explicit about your needs. Short of that, you may need to be creative to make the room work.

Let's look at some factors that will help you determine your required room setup. For example, how many participants will you have in the learning experience? What type of activities will the participants be engaged in? Group activities require rounds or team tables. How many teams are you going to have? How many members to a team? Will each team require a flipchart or other audiovisual equipment? How much facilitated discussion and participant interaction will you have? What physical limitations will the room have? These include narrow versus wide floor plans, pillars, folding doors, irregular walls, amount of windows versus wall space, and wall surfaces for hanging visuals on the walls.

Your Space
How you set up the front of the room and the rest of the room is a reflection of your style and comfort. Your first decision is determining where the front of the room is. Given the existence of windows, sunlight, doors, and refreshments, you need to determine where the front of the room will be.

When considering your workspace, it is recommended that you use an open style. An open style requires just a front table to hold your materials and a side table for handouts.

In the open setup, there is no podium or stand. Although a podium gives you something to hide behind or cling to with white knuckles if you get nervous, it also creates a barrier between you and your participants. Should you ever use a podium or lectern? Rarely, if ever. Podiums and lecterns are fine for presentations, but they are not conducive to facilitated learning. It is far better to move around and interact with the learners. Podiums restrict facilitator movement, limit learner interaction with the facilitator, cause the learners to take passive roles, and erect a physical barrier between you and the learners.

You may want to use one or two flipcharts, placed to the side. If you are using a screen, it should be mounted either directly behind you or to the side.

Screen mounting can be a real issue. In some cases, you have no options because screens are permanently mounted. If the screen is directly behind you, be aware that your physical body can block the learners' view. Therefore, you will need to move to the side. If the screen is in the corner, learners have a better view and there is less likelihood of you being a visual barrier. However, depending on how far back and the angle, learners seated on the same side that the screen is located may have some trouble seeing the screen. You will need to set the screen once the rest of the room is set.

Noted

If at all possible, your screen should hang at a slant; that is, the top of the screen should hang a few inches further away from the wall than the bottom portion. This technique eliminates the keystone effect, which is a distortion of your images caused by a flat screen hung at a straight angle.

Types of Learner Setups

Rounds. The term *rounds* refers to a setup that uses multiple round tables at which learners are seated (figure 4-1). The rounds are placed throughout the room for maximum visibility. The facilitator is at the front with the required tables. Flipcharts can be placed beside the rounds for group work. The center rounds will have their flipcharts on the side of the room. In some cases, you may not have actual round

Think About This

If you use Microsoft PowerPoint, also use a remote control device. In many cases, the computer is placed on the front table or on a podium. Having to stay close to the computer to change slides can restrict your movements. Using a remote will allow you freedom of movement.

tables; you might have small rectangular tables instead. In this case, you can put two tables together for added seating and work space. You could also develop the T-effect by placing two tables at a 90-degree angle to each other.

Rounds are great to use when you are going to do a great deal of small group work. It allows easy group inter-action, creates a friendly and open envi-ronment, and provides a large surface to work on. This layout also allows the

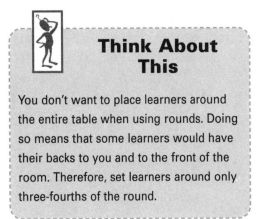

facilitator to work the room by walking among the rounds. Rounds are good for group sizes of 16 to 24, with four to six people at a round.

Rounds do require a fairly large room to allow for the tables, flipcharts, and movement. If the room is too small and everyone is crowded together, you lose some of the benefits of that open environment and freedom of movement. Another issue to watch out for is learning visibility. Rounds, if not properly set or if too many, can cause some learners to have difficulty seeing your work at the front.

U-Shaped Setup. This setup has two sets of tables parallel to each other, making two sides of the U, while another set of tables is horizontal (at 90 degrees to the par-allel tables) at the back (figure 4-2). The inside of the U is open. There may be a facilitator's table at the front, but it does not close the space.

The number of tables in a U-shaped setup depends on three factors:

▸ total number of learners; the optimum is usually 12 to 18
▸ number of learners that can be seated at an individual table comfortably
▸ size of the room.

The U-shaped configuration is good for allowing learners and small (two or three learners) teams to interact with each other. This setup also allows the facilita-tor freedom of movement within the U to build rapport and enhance communica-tion. This configuration also provides good visibility of the front of the room.

Figure 4-1. Room set up in rounds.

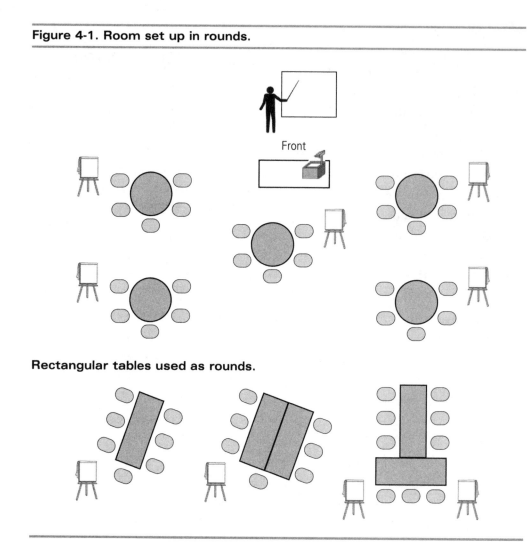

Front

Rectangular tables used as rounds.

The U-shape must fit the room. If the room is narrow, you may have a U that is too narrow and too deep, which can actually hinder communication because the back table and learners are too far from the front learners to effectively communicate. If the room is too narrow, learners have a difficult time walking around the outside of the U. Finally, the setup is not conducive for having learners work in groups of more than three or four. If you want to do teams of five or six, the members must move to another part of the room. You will then have workstations with flipcharts for the teams.

Figure 4-2. U-shaped setup.

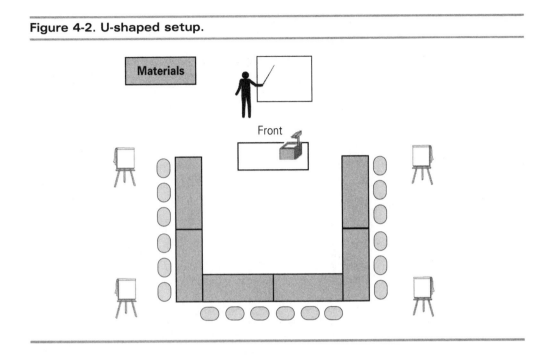

Conference Setup. The conference setup (figure 4-3), which involves several learners sitting around a conference table, is similar to the U-shaped setup.

The table shape can be oblong or rectangular. You then have the option of sitting at the head, indicating a leadership position or joining the group by sitting in another seat. Although good for more formal presentations, the conference setup does not work well for facilitating learning experiences. It is difficult to have teamwork, limits your choice of media, presents a problem of storing handouts, and hinders your movement among the learners.

Classroom Setup. The classroom configuration (figure 4-4) has been the traditional setup for the last century. Here, rows of tables and chairs are all facing the facilitator, who is standing at the front. Usually, the facilitator works from a table with a side table for materials.

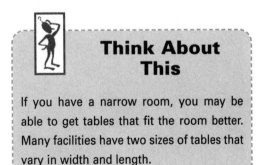

Think About This

If you have a narrow room, you may be able to get tables that fit the room better. Many facilities have two sizes of tables that vary in width and length.

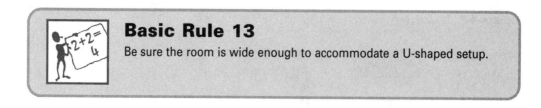

Basic Rule 13

Be sure the room is wide enough to accommodate a U-shaped setup.

Figure 4-3. Conference setups.

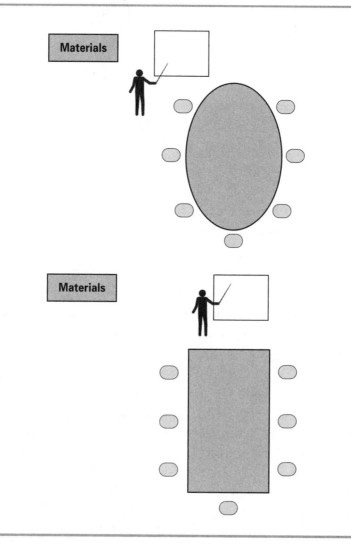

Figure 4-4. Classroom setup.

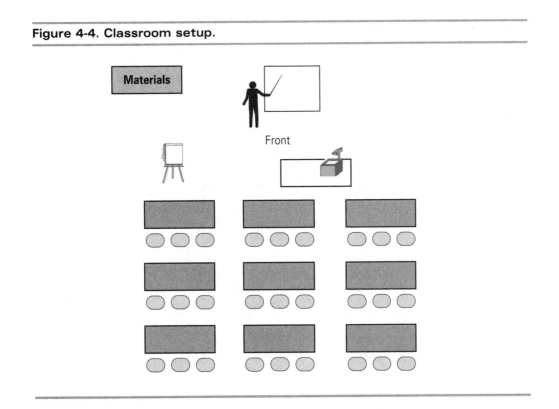

The classroom setup is not recommended for facilitating learning experiences. By its very nature, this setup places the facilitator as the focal point of the attention—quite the opposite of the goal of facilitated learning in which learners are to play the primary role while the facilitator guides the learning.

Classroom setups do not allow for teamwork or good group communication and discussion. There is also the problem of visibility: Learners in back rows cannot see the front of the room, and the facilitator cannot see those in the back of the room. Learners can't see and talk with each other. This is especially true if the room is deep and narrow. Add a column or open panel doors and you really have a problem.

Chevron Setup. This setup is like a classroom setup except that the tables are angled. It has rows of tables, aligned one in front of the other, which are placed at an angle, forming a V-shape (figure 4-5).

Figure 4-5. Chevron setup.

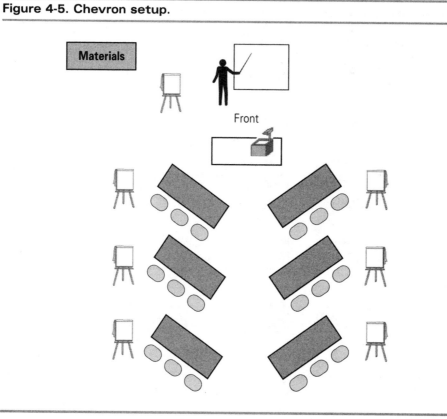

As with rounds, this setup allows the facilitator to move into the group for better interaction. It also allows for small group teamwork using triads at a table. The chevron setup can accommodate larger groups and still have some visibility of the front. This setup is also conducive to using several forms of media, but it does have some drawbacks.

As is true for the classroom configuration, this setup restricts good interaction among the learners. Who likes to look at and talk to the back of another's head? There can still be a problem for those in the back seeing the front and hearing all comments.

Hybrid or Fishbone Setup. This setup combines the U with the chevron and is used when there are too many learners for a good U and where the room is wide enough to accommodate the breadth of tables. In this setup, you set the U and then develop the chevron within the U (figure 4-6).

Figure 4-6. Hybrid or fishbone setup.

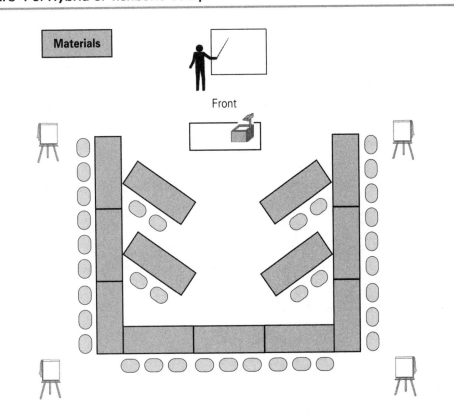

This setup allows the facilitator to move within the setup to increase communication. It also has better group communication than the chevron alone. With larger groups, it allows the learners to be close together, increasing facilitator and learner visibility. Teamwork is a little easier because those inside the U can work with those beside them and/or behind them. Flipcharts will need to be placed outside the U. However, there is still the issue of some learners looking at the back of the heads of others.

Basic Rule 14

Your room setup should support learning and accommodate the size of the room.

A Reality Check on Room Setup

Here are some tips to help you manage the realities of setups:

- Always arrive at least an hour early on the first day. In hotels, this buffer gives you a chance to check the room and have it set or reset the room under your guidance.
- If you can't make setup changes before the beginning of the learning experience, make the changes at lunch or before the start of the next day.
- If using a company training room, make sure it can accommodate your desired setup. If not, change rooms.
- If you use breakout rooms, make sure they have the equipment and supplies required and that they are in close proximity to your room.
- Be sure the room can accommodate your media. Not all rooms have a sufficient wall space (due to windows) for projection or hanging flipchart pages. Some rooms are not equipped or configured for computer projection. If a room is narrow and deep, the learners may be too far away to read your prepared flipchart or wallboards.
- Avoid using a room with columns. They can be a logistical nightmare. If you must use a room with columns, try to make the seating arrangement fit within the columns, although this may make the usable part of the room narrower.
- Determine the amount of wall space you need for posting teams' work and some of your flipchart work as well as wallboards or posters.
- Windows can be a problem. There is always the issue of learners gazing outside, especially if it is a fine spring day! In addition, too much natural light can cause media problems. If you have to live with windows, be sure you can close some blinds or drapes. Although you don't want a drab room, too many open windows can detract from the learning.
- Be sure the room is not located in a high-traffic area; this is especially true for programs delivered in outside facilities.
- When leaving the room for lunch and breaks, be sure you can secure the room. You don't want participants' laptop computers and other possessions to disappear.
- If the course covers several days, be sure the cleaning crew does not throw out the work that has been done. More than one facilitator has lost a good day's work when all the charts have been removed from the walls or team tables.

Other Physical Environment Factors

Temperature. The room must be comfortable—not too hot or too cold. Keep this in mind: the more bodies in the room, the higher the temperature will be. Check the room thermostat and adjust it accordingly. If the temperature is centrally controlled, find out how to make adjustments before the program begins. If the temperature cannot be under your control, the best alternative is to find another room. If that is not possible, and the room will remain cold, let the learners know that they should bring a jacket or sweater. If the room will remain hot and you can't change rooms, be sure there is water available, and consider changing the course schedule to use the room when it is at its coolest.

Peripheral Materials and Methods. Having posters on the wall and handouts on the table that are relevant to your course content makes the room seem less sterile and gives arriving learners something to look at and talk about. Providing tablets and writing utensils is a nice touch. You also want to have nametags or name tent cards available so the learners can identify themselves for you and for each other. If your course content includes equipment or job site materials, having samples of those on the tables enhances learning.

Some facilitators put small toys or puzzles on the tables. These provide opportunities for learner interaction, keep faster learners occupied while waiting for slower learners to complete an activity, and are important for kinesthetic learners—they will actually play with the items during the learning event to stay engaged with the content. However, you must manage this. Some learners play with these toys to the point of being a distraction.

Refreshments. Having water available is important, and having other refreshments, such as coffee and soft drinks, and even food is a nice touch. Consider the following tips regarding refreshments:

- ▶ Have caffeinated and caffeine-free beverages available and always have water on hand.
- ▶ Candy is a nice touch to have on tables; hard candy is better than soft because there's less opportunity for mess, and they can also help suppress coughing if need be.
- ▶ Plan to have beverages replenished regularly not only to keep an adequate supply, but to keep coffee fresh as well.

▸ If providing food, don't provide only high-sugar items such as donuts, pastries, and cookies. Some learners want and need low-sugar items such as bagels and fruit. Also, consider a high-protein item like cheese cubes.

Preparing Yourself

There is no worse feeling for a facilitator than to enter the learning environment unprepared. Three items that have been addressed include knowing as much as possible about the learners, knowing your course content, and knowing the leader's guide with learning activities. Subsequent chapters discuss knowing your activities, sequence, and pace. And here are even more:

▸ Get a good night's sleep before the learning event.

▸ Do some stretching exercises prior to entering the room.

▸ Walk around the room and make sure that everything can be seen from every seat. Check for loose cords on the floor and other hazards.

▸ Memorize the first few sentences you will say.

▸ Practice with the audiovisual equipment. (This point cannot be repeated too many times!)

▸ Choose comfortable clothing (especially shoes) that makes you feel good and look professional. A nice guideline is to dress one step above your audience. For example, if your audience wears work uniforms on a plant floor, you might want to wear khakis and a golf shirt. If your audience is business casual, you may want to wear a tie or pantsuit.

▸ Keep water with lemon available in case your throat gets dry.

▸ Breathe deeply before you begin talking; if your breath gets short during the first few minutes (hyperventilation), breathe deeply in through your nose and out through your mouth a few times. You can even do this surreptitiously while a participant is making a comment or asking a question.

▸ Keep your knees slightly flexed; if you lock your knees, your circulation may become impeded causing you to become light-headed.

▸ Smile, relax, and have fun!

Greeting the Learners

Be in your room a suitable time before the start of the course so you can greet learners as they arrive. Try to arrive at least a half hour ahead of the start time. On the first day, you need to arrive earlier to be sure the room is arranged properly and to distribute material, hang wallboards and posters, and check the audiovisual equipment, and make other preparations. Shake hands, welcome the learner, and introduce yourself. Show the learner where to sit, what materials are available, and where the refreshments are located.

Basic Rule 15

Always greet the learners as they arrive. If you are still doing some preparation, stop what you are doing to greet them, and then return to your preparation work. Plan to finish any final preparation work at least 10–15 minutes before the course's start, so you can chat with learners and make yourself comfortable as well.

Your Physical Presence

Remember at the beginning of the book when the assumption was presented that you already possess basic presentation skills? This is where much of your physical presence comes in to play. Here are some things to focus on and remember:

- Modulate your voice by changing your pitch and volume appropriately. Monotone puts people to sleep. Also, watch out for the rising inflection some people put at the end of a sentence—it makes every sentence sound like a question!
- Use a physical stance that feels comfortable for you. Some tips: Place your feet firmly on the floor; flex your knees slightly; maintain erect posture; keep your hands away from your face and out of your pockets; watch out for distracting physical habits. You may want to videotape yourself and watch for distractions you may not be aware of (for example, playing with a marker or paperclip while speaking, too many gestures, not enough gestures).
- Take your time; don't speak or move too fast. Use a pace that feels comfortable.
- Make eye contact with all the participants as you speak.

Learners will mirror your physical energy, sometimes at an unconscious level. Model the energy level you want to create with your posture, tone of voice, and physical movement. If you sit down or lean against a table, or in some other way model low energy, they will do it too, by leaning back in their seats, not participating, and so forth. Don't allow yourself to droop physically—especially right after lunch. The learners will follow your example, and you'll all be snoozing!

Basic Rule 16

Model the energy level that you want to create in the learners.

Opening Activities

When your course begins, the first things that happen set the tone for the rest of the time you are with your learners. It's tempting and feels "organized" to the facilitator to make the first activity informational, i.e., the facilitator does the talking and it's all about "Welcome, here's who I am, here's our schedule and agenda, here's where the restrooms and smoking areas are, and so on." However, this is not the best way to begin.

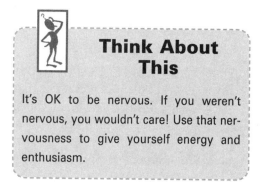

Think About This

It's OK to be nervous. If you weren't nervous, you wouldn't care! Use that nervousness to give yourself energy and enthusiasm.

When you start the program in a way that forces the learners to be passive, you set the tone for passivity for the rest of the course, making it more difficult to engage the participants. Additionally, starting a program in this way puts the focus on you, not them, and that breaks the cardinal rule: It's about them! Instead, get the learners active and involved with each other in the first activity. Not only will you set the tone for engagement and involvement early on, but you also will increase the learners' comfort level with each other.

In addition to setting a participative tone, good opening activities help the learners relax and become receptive to learning. Your opening activity can help break the ice and set the tone for sharing. For example, you can go around the room and ask all the participants how many years of experience they have. Add up the numbers on a flipchart page to see how much collective experience resides in the room. Another

Basic Rule 17

Begin a learning event with an activity.

idea is to have the learners introduce themselves. One active way to do this is to have learner pairs interview each other and then have each person introduce his or her partner to the group.

Or, conduct some quick, on-the-spot polls, surveys, or discussions that can give you more information about the learners' backgrounds and skills. You can also introduce some group activities to gather the learners' expectations of the course. Then, when you present the agenda, you can refer to their comments.

When your opening activity is over, and learners are relaxed and comfortable, that's the time to launch into the introductory material, sometimes called housekeeping items.

Important considerations for choosing your opening activity include these:

> Make sure the comfort level is a good match for the learners at hand.

> The shorter your course, the shorter your opening activity should be. For a four-hour course, your opening activity might take 15 minutes; in a multiple-day course, it might take two hours. A five-day course might have an opening activity that takes the entire first morning. It's your call to decide what needs to happen to set the stage for your content and for learning.

> If your learners already know each other, focus the opening activity on content or on their expectations, not just on introductions.

> Watch out for the silliness factor: Depending on your audience and organization culture, you might not want to go very far in the opening activity. As

Noted

Some learners may come to your course preoccupied and distracted by work or personal issues. If you know that ahead of time, your opening activity can focus on helping them set aside those distractions and be more open to learning. Here are a couple of ideas that can help. Try developing an "issue chart" or "parking lot" flipchart or whiteboard and let the learners know that when issues come up that are distracting for the moment, they will be "parked" there. Make sure to address these issues when appropriate during the course of the program. Another idea is to ask learners to make a personal list of all the distractions that are on their minds and have them fold up the lists so they remain private. Then, collect the lists in an envelope and tell the learners you will keep their distractions safe until the course is over. When they leave, they can pick them up on their way out.

Think About This

Several books and articles listed in the Additional Resources section offer suggestions for icebreaker activities (as well as other types of learning activities) with instructions for facilitation.

long as you create active involvement and participation, that's OK. Even a small group discussion in which they share, then a large group in which you collect what they shared, is still participative.

Ground rules are behavioral expectations that the facilitators and learners have of each other to support the learning. Developing ground rules can be an excellent opening activity. Depending on your assessment of which activity will work best, you can

- present a list of proposed ground rules and facilitate an activity in which the learners react to and revise them
- facilitate an activity in which the learners propose their own ground rules and then come to consensus or vote on them.

When the ground rules are established, post them so they are always visible. And, the learners should decide on a way to "call each other" on the ground rules when one is broken. Depending on the formality of the environment, the "calling" method can be as low key as the learners simply committing to point it out verbally, all the way to throwing paper wads or Nerf balls at the offender.

Noted

When you introduce yourself, should you make a big deal out of your background and qualifications? No. To establish some immediate credibility, you can put a short biography in the learners' materials to be read at their leisure. Additional credibility is generated by your facilitation and expertise as the course progresses. Too much emphasis on your background makes the learning event about you.

Many of your ground rules can be tailored to the organizational environment. Some typical ground rules that work in many environments include the following:

▶ All learners participate actively.

▶ No question is a dumb question.

▶ Return punctually after breaks and lunch.

▶ Turn off or set cell phones and pagers to silent mode and return calls during breaks.

▶ Challenge each other respectfully.

▶ No interruptions or side conversations are to be tolerated.

▶ Ask questions and make comments that will help make the learning yours.

▶ Everyone has the right to pass.

▶ Discussions that occur in the room stay in the room to maintain confidentiality.

Personalizing Your Facilitation

Another aspect of getting the learning off to a good start is personalizing the course and materials so that they reflect your expertise and style as a facilitator. The more the materials fit you, and the more comfortable you are, the more conducive the climate is to learning. Personalization allows you to capitalize on your own talents.

Your Materials

One aspect of personalization is simply reviewing the materials and knowing what comes first, next, and so on. Identify the content that you think is most critical and plan how you will emphasize it. Identify the content areas that you want to expand on when you get to that part. Think about and prepare for the most likely learner questions and comments.

Examples and Stories

Prepare examples and war stories from your own experiences that will illustrate content points. Practice your telling of these items so that you are prepared to emphasize the points that are most illustrative. You can even leave out part of it and then tell the rest of the story later, or you can ask the group, "What do you think happened next?"

Winging it with examples and stories doesn't work. You can get off schedule in a big way. If you select a story or example to tell on the spot, you might be stealing your thunder for a later content point. You might get to the end and discover that the main point isn't really relevant to the content at hand. Some facilitators even get to the end of a spur-of-the-moment story and realize that not only does it not make a point, but also that the punch line is offensive. Think through your telling of examples and stories.

Basic Rule 18

Don't wing it when it comes to your stories and examples. Plan ahead: Make sure the stories and examples are in alignment with the learning objectives, and rehearse them so that they flow smoothly.

Humor

Speaking of punch lines, humor in general must be addressed. Appropriate jokes and funny stories can be very effective in making a point and in establishing a comfortable climate. Following are tips for using humor, jokes, and funny stories:

- The humorous item must be relevant to the learning and content at hand. Telling a story or joke just for fun takes the learning off track.
- Practice telling it so you know what to emphasize or exaggerate, and so you don't forget the punch line.
- Make sure your joke or story is clean. Perhaps this cautionary note seems obvious, but for some facilitators, it isn't. Using even mild curse words is offensive to some learners, and it makes you look unprofessional. And, don't make the mistake of thinking that, if your audience swears, you can too. Part of your role is to model professional behavior.

The other caveat that should be obvious is don't use jokes or stories that stereotype racial groups, age groups, ethnic groups, the sexes, or other characteristics of people that are not related to the learning experience. And, that includes your own group, whatever it may be! It's not OK to make jokes about your own ethnicity, age,

Basic Rule 19

With humor, when in doubt—don't.

sex, or whatever because not all folks who are like you will agree with you. And, joking about one's own group doesn't give license to joke about other groups!

Use humor to be inclusive, not exclusive. All the learners might not get the joke if you make a humorous reference to a current event or a current movie, for example. Be prepared to explain it, or don't use the reference at all. One of the worst things that a facilitator can do is exclude some of the learners from the process.

One last point about stories and humor: If telling jokes and stories isn't your long suit, it's perfectly OK not to do it. There are other personalization methods that might work better for you. Some people are simply not good storytellers: They are too fast or too slow, or they forget the punch line!

Take advantage of your own uniqueness. After all, the word *personalize* means that you can do something that comes from your own talents to enhance the learning. Are you a juggler, an amateur magician, a poet, a songwriter, or an artist? The potential list goes on and on of talents that you can use to make learning points. Here's an example: A facilitator was a professional rock musician in a former life. In a course about teamwork, he divided his class into small groups and gave them all percussion instruments (triangles, maracas, finger cymbals, and so forth). He taught each small group a specific rhythm with their instruments and allowed them to practice. Then, he had one group begin with their rhythm and had each group add their rhythms one by one until the whole room was rocking with an orchestrated percussion beat. What better way to make learning points about teamwork and synergy?

Basic Rule 20

Use your unique talents and skills to personalize and enhance learning.

Getting It Done

This chapter discussed the many factors involved in preparing for a learning event and establishing the learning environment. Now, in exercise 4-1, you have an opportunity to check yourself using a checklist and to make plans to accomplish the items that you haven't yet completed.

In the next chapter, you will get into the learning event itself, and you'll learn tips, techniques, and strategies for facilitating various types of learning activities.

Exercise 4-1. Are you ready to facilitate a learning event?

For the planning list below, check yes or no to indicate whether you have performed the task. If yes, summarize the results or findings; if no, list the actions you will take to complete the task.

Facilitation Planning Task	Completed?	Results/Actions to Take
I have studied and assessed learner characteristics.	☐ Yes ☐ No	
I have built strategies into the facilitation to learn more about the learners.	☐ Yes ☐ No	
I have planned facilitation tactics to accommodate learner characteristics.	☐ Yes ☐ No	
I have identified the optimal room setup and the potential need for breakout rooms.	☐ Yes ☐ No	
I have identified and planned for physical environment factors (locations of audiovisual equipment, charts, screen, lighting, wall space, room security, and room temperature).	☐ Yes ☐ No	
I have planned appropriate peripheral materials and supporting components (posters, writing utensils, toys/puzzles, refreshments).	☐ Yes ☐ No	
I am prepared physically and mentally (rested, ready to model appropriate energy level, and know what I will do to calm my nerves).	☐ Yes ☐ No	
I am prepared professionally (know what I will say in the beginning; have examined my stance, posture, voice, and physical presence; have chosen appropriate and comfortable clothing).	☐ Yes ☐ No	
I have planned opening components (ready to greet the learners and create their comfort zone; opening activity is planned to set the tone for participative involvement).	☐ Yes ☐ No	
I have identified and planned ways to personalize facilitation and materials to reflect me and my uniqueness.	☐ Yes ☐ No	

5

Facilitating Learning
Activities

■ ■

 What's Inside This Chapter

In this chapter, you'll learn:

▶ Three main types of learning activities
▶ Three main types of skill practices
▶ Ways to confirm the choice of learning activity by aligning it with learning objectives
▶ How to meet varied learning preference needs in learning activities
▶ About the characteristics and purposes of transfer activities.

The key to good facilitation in general is practice, practice, and more practice. When you turn your attention to facilitating specific kinds of learning activities, this advice is true as well, but, in addition, you must also plan, plan, and plan. Nothing affects the potential success or failure of a learning activity more than how well you plan the activity by thinking through each aspect of the activity ahead of time so that the facilitation will go smoothly.

Types of Learning Activities

Three main categories of learning activities are discussed here: content/knowledge/comprehension activities, structured exercises, and skill practice. Within each category are multiple and varied methods for facilitation.

1. Content/Knowledge/Comprehension Activities

These types of activities are intended to disseminate information, increase awareness, and assist participants in understanding concepts. The foundation of all skills is knowledge, and learners must know before they can do. These activities apply to learners who don't have any or very little background in the content of the lesson or course.

Content/knowledge/comprehension activities are characterized by relative passivity on the part of the participants (they are usually listening, reading, or observing without interacting); greater focus on the facilitator (who must deliver the content because participants don't know it); and (usually) individual rather than group work. Examples of content/knowledge/comprehension learning activities include

- lecture
- reading books or handouts
- videos/DVDs/films, slides, overhead transparencies
- prework
- PowerPoint presentations
- note taking
- self-assessments such as quizzes and checklists.

Think About This

Never lecture for more than 20 minutes. With lectures, not only do you lose your participants' attention, but also during a lecture they are passive, not active. When they cannot engage with the content, they do not learn as much of it.

2. Structured Exercises

Structured exercises constitute the discovery bridge between knowledge and skills. In structured exercises, the learners work together to understand and use content at a deeper level than simply comprehension: They learn variations of the content, how to use and apply it, and how to make it their own. Learners are more active and involved than they are with content/knowledge/comprehension activities. The focus is on the learners, and the facilitator's role is that of organizer, monitor, and guide.

Structured exercises are used with learners who have some knowledge of the desired content and are ready for more depth and concept application. Sometimes the supporting knowledge has been acquired earlier in the same course. In other instances, the learners have the content and experience when they walk in. In this case, the first type of exercise used is often a structured exercise. The learner groups are given questions to answer or a problem to solve, and, in the process, the new content is discovered.

Noted

What can you do in structured exercises with a mixed group of some novices and some who have preexisting knowledge? This special case is discussed in chapter 6.

Here are some examples of structured exercises listed in order of increasing learner involvement:

- ▶ *Solo work:* Learners are given an assignment to work on by themselves (such as a questionnaire to complete or a problem to analyze) and then discuss with others.
- ▶ *Guided discussion or question-and-answer session:* The facilitator asks the group planned questions designed to get them to wrestle with content at a deeper level. As they answer the questions, the facilitator summarizes their content, adds his or her own content, plays devil's advocate to drive for deeper content or application, and guides the discussion to the next question.
- ▶ *Small group discussion:* Small learner groups are given a topic to discuss or questions to answer; the learners work together and then present their results to the larger group.
- ▶ *Group inquiry:* The learners are provided with content, and they work together to identify questions they have about the content.
- ▶ *Information search:* The learners are given reference materials and must search them for answers to questions presented by the facilitator. In a blended learning experience (a combination of face-to-face learning and e-learning), the search may involve using the Internet to conduct searches or to download information.

- *Small group assignment or problem solving:* Small groups of learners are given a problem to solve, a situation to analyze, a list of principles or guidelines to develop in response to a problem, or some similar type of exercise.

- *Peer teaching:* Small groups of learners study the material and then teach it to the other participants or groups within the class. Choosing the teaching methodology is part of the activity and is left up to the groups.

- *Games:* A popular game (Jeopardy, Bingo, Concentration) can be adapted to assist learners in remembering, comprehending, and applying content that has been presented.

- *Debriefing session:* The facilitator leads a large group guided discussion after a structured exercise or skill practice is complete; it is designed to close the gaps in the learning, summarize the main points, and help the learners apply the content to the job.

3. Skill Practice

Once the learners have mastered knowledge to the depth that they need, the next part of the learning is skill practice. Skill practice is exactly what it says it is—the actual practice of the skill. If the skill is driving a car, then the skill practice is actually driving a car (or a simulator). If the skill is conducting a job interview or making a sales presentation, then the skill practice is conducting a mock interview or sales presentation. If the skill is analyzing a situation and making recommendations, then the skill practice is analyzing a case situation and making recommendations. In other words, skill practice is the actual performance of the skill, adjusted when necessary for the learning environment. A detailed feedback instrument accompanies the skill practice. There are three types of skill practices, as shown in table 5-1.

Transfer Activities

Transfer activities are specifically intended to support the learners' ability to transfer their learning back to the job and apply it there. Transfer activities can be any one of the types described previously, but they are specifically targeted toward successful on-the-job application. Examples of transfer activities include

- *Action planning:* This activity consists of solo work on a plan of action to apply skills. The action planning can be done at the end of the course or

Table 5-1. Three types of skill practices.

	Psychomotor Skills	Intellectual Skills	Interpersonal Skills
Definition	Actual physical skills that the learners must perform	Skills that learners perform using judgment and mental processes	Skills that learners perform while interacting with other people
Examples	Drive a car in rain, create a spreadsheet, repair a hard drive	Decide what to do at various traffic signals, evaluate a report, troubleshoot a process, analyze a budget, develop an account plan	Resolve conflict after a fender bender, conduct a job interview, give constructive feedback, provide coaching
Activities	Demonstration and hands-on practice: Learners see the skill performed, they try it and receive feedback according to criteria for how each step should be followed.	Case or problem solving: Learners in groups (sometimes singly) are given a situation or problem and work to solve it. Sometimes it is a real business problem, and learners present their results to management. Many transfer activities (e.g., action planning, barriers, and strategies) fall into this category.	Behavior modeling or role playing in which learners act out the situation with each other: Can be a videotaped model/demonstration followed by practice; instructor-led; instructor interaction with the learner(s); scripted; fishbowl (in which two role players perform with the rest of the class observing); and free form (in which role players are given the general parameters of the situation and are free to improvise over and above that)
Feedback	Process checklist	Quality criteria checklist	Behavioral process checklist for behavior modeling or a quality criteria checklist for role playing

Reprinted with permission from Deb Tobey LLC, 2003.

used intermittently throughout the course so learners apply as they move through the content. Action plans can also be developed in partnership with the learners' managers.

▶ *Performance contracting:* The learner and his or her manager can prepare an advanced planning document to help prepare for the program and ensure that the course content transfers to the job. The performance contract focuses on how the course content will be used on the job, required resources and support, and identification of barriers and enablers to transfer and how to address them. It also serves as a pre-course organizer.

▶ *Application discussion:* The emphasis during this guided discussion is on opportunities for application back on the job.

▶ *Barriers and strategies:* During this structured activity, learners identify barriers to application back on the job and then strategize to overcome the barriers.

▶ *Enablers and strategies:* This structured activity helps learners identify forces in the organization that support the use of the new knowledge and skills on the job and strategize to strengthen those forces.

▶ *Structured note taking:* Using "applying the concepts" format, participants make a quick note of the topic or comment and how it can be applied to the job. This document is later referred to during action planning and follow-up.

▶ *Manager presentation:* Managers are invited to be on a panel that hears participants' presentations and makes comments on their job relevance.

▶ *Case studies:* Based on actual organizational situations and data, learners solve the case and then discuss the relevancy of the solution to the organization.

▶ *Team projects:* Learners are given an actual corporate or business unit problem or opportunity. They then develop strategies to address the problem or opportunity and present it to a senior management panel for discussion.

▶ *Letters home:* Learners write letters to their managers presenting what they learned in a particular area and how they want to use that knowledge or skill on the job. They indicate that upon their return they want a meeting to discuss the implementation of the actions. Then, the letters are mailed.

The most important thing to remember about transfer activities is that they are always focused on helping learners apply what they have learned back in their own job contexts.

Planning Considerations for Learning Activities

What must you keep in mind as you plan the activities that will engage your learners in an active way? First, you have to choose an appropriate learning activity and then you have to be sure that the selected learning activity will meet the needs of all three types of learning preferences (visual, auditory, and kinesthetic).

Confirming Learning Activity Choice

Your choice of learning activity is a design decision based on the course's learning objectives. What do the learners need to be able to do (terminal learning objective) when they leave the class? Structured exercises and skill practice activities will support the learners' abilities to actually perform skills. What do they need to know (enabling learning objective) to be able to do it? Content/knowledge/comprehension activities provide the understanding and information that they will need before they can actually perform.

You must confirm the designer's learning activity choices by revisiting the learning objectives and ensuring that there is an appropriately chosen learning activity that corresponds to each learning objective.

For example: You're preparing to facilitate a driving class for novice drivers. One of the terminal learning objectives is: *Decide on the appropriate action when faced with a traffic sign or signal* (something the learners must be able to *do*). You must check to see that there is a learning activity that involves practicing the mental skill of deciding what action to take at a traffic sign/signal. You also must check that there is an enabling learning objective and corresponding content and learning activity that will provide knowledge of traffic signs and signals (what they need to *know* before they can *do*). In this case, an enabling learning objective might be: *Explain the meaning of the eight most commonly used traffic signs and signals,* which could be supported by a content/knowledge/comprehension activity.

Basic Rule 21
All learning activities must support appropriate learning objectives.

Think About This

In some courses, a knowledge set might be a prerequisite for attendance in the course; for example, learners attending the driving course must already know the meanings of traffic signs. That would make a content/knowledge/comprehension activity unnecessary in the class because they come to the class with the knowledge already mastered, assuming they really have mastered the prerequisites. In any event—whether they come with the knowledge or they learn it in the class—they must still *know* before they *do*.

Meeting the Needs of Different Learning Preferences

Chapter 3 discussed the characteristics of the three main learning preferences: visual, auditory, and kinesthetic. That chapter also covered the types of learning activities and media that work well with different learning styles. It is important to acknowledge that people with different learning preferences and styles are engaged differently, depending on their preference/style and the activity you've chosen.

You must think ahead about the types of activities and materials that will be used and make sure to accommodate all learning preferences/styles. Three guidelines help you in addressing learning preferences and styles:

1. *Two out of three, every time:* Use techniques that appeal to at least two of the three learning preferences in every activity. For example, if you present instructions for an activity verbally and put the instructions on a flipchart or handout, you have hit the auditory and visual preferences at the same time. In many cases, you can hit all three preferences.

2. *Change up often:* By transitioning to a new topic or activity (or both) often and by changing the type of activity, you'll hit different combinations of preferences and styles throughout the course. In this way, people are in and out of their comfort zones throughout the course. This effort leads to participants' willingness to participate and be outside of their comfort zones for a while because the expectation has been established that they will soon be back in it. Other considerations regarding changing up are discussed in chapter 6 in the sections on pace and sequence.

3. *Watch out for your own style:* The activities you are most comfortable facilitating are most likely the ones that match your own learning style. If you're not careful, you'll tend to use those activities too much. Effective facilitators take themselves out of their own comfort zones and choose to facilitate all kinds of learning activities so that all kinds of learning styles are accommodated.

The example in figure 5-1 illustrates a simple outline for a lesson in the driving class example. The outline demonstrates alignment of learning activities with learning objectives and selection of activities to accommodate varied learning styles. The assumption, which drives the order of activities in this example, is that the learners have very little background and knowledge in driving. This outline is not something that you would show your learners; rather, it is a planning tool for you to illustrate the thought process that supports the choice of activities. For your learners, you might take the column labeled "Learning Activities" and produce it as an agenda.

Special Case: Closing Activities

Do you recall in chapter 4 when special needs for opening activities were discussed? Closing activities need the same amount of special attention because of the opportunity to wrap up all the loose ends and because the closing will be the last thing the learners remember.

Just as in opening activities, the length of your closing activity depends on the length of the course itself. For a four-hour course, your closing activity might take 15 minutes; for a weeklong course, it might take two hours. A good closing activity has the following goals:

▶ Review and summarize the main points of the course content.
▶ Emphasize the most important content points.
▶ Point out learners' progress since the course's beginning.
▶ Address any "parking lot" issues or questions that remain.
▶ Begin the task of transfer by focusing on back-on-the-job application of the skills in the activities and discussions.
▶ Complete administrative work: evaluations, addresses (if you will be sending the participants follow-up material), and a business card exchange if appropriate.

Figure 5-1. Example outline for a driving class.

Lesson 3: Driving for Novices: Traffic Signs and Signals

Learning Objective	Learning Activities	Type of Activity	Learning Styles Addressed
Explain the meaning of the eight most-used traffic signs and signals	Lecture on traffic signs and signals with handouts and slides	Content/knowledge/ comprehension	Visual Auditory
Identify the eight most-used traffic signs and signals by shape and color	Self-quiz: handout in which learners fill in the blanks on a diagram of traffic signs	Content/knowledge/ comprehension	Visual Kinesthetic
Apply knowledge of traffic signs and signals to various situations	Structured exercise: "What would you do if . . . ?" Traffic scenarios that they work together in small groups to solve; computer simulation	Structured exercise	Auditory (Kinesthetic as well if they make flipcharts during the activity or engage the simulation)
Take appropriate action when faced with a traffic sign or signal	Practice: Drive in a car or simulator to a variety of signs and act on them with instructor in passenger seat	Skill practice	Visual Auditory Kinesthetic
Apply traffic signs and signals skills to future driving activities	Debrief: Large group discussion with planned questions on how the practice went; challenges and things they will do differently in the future	Guided discussion	Auditory

Never cut short or rush your closing activity! If you must adjust on the fly, do it earlier in the course. If the learners don't get the full experience of your closing activity, what they remember is being rushed or the feeling that something was missing. In particular, your opportunities to support job application and skill transfer will be lost.

Think About This

Opening and closing activities must meet the requirements for good learning activities in general: alignment with the course learning objectives and use of techniques that support varied learning preferences and styles. The course closing is your last opportunity to personalize your facilitation by leaving the learners with a story, object lesson, visual, or some other technique that will make the course memorable and meaningful to them—and to you—and to tie up the learning with a big ribbon!

Getting It Done

This chapter presented the many variables that must be planned for before a learning event, and managed during the learning event. Exercise 5-1 will support your analysis and preparation for facilitation.

Exercise 5-1. Are you ready to facilitate a learning event?

Use the following worksheet to review course components as you prepare to facilitate.

1. Check each of the learning activities that are built into your course by putting an X in the space next to it.

Content/Knowledge/Comprehension

_____ Lecture
_____ Reading: books, handouts
_____ Videos/DVDs/films, slides, overheads
_____ Prework
_____ PowerPoint presentations
_____ Note taking
_____ Self-assessments (e.g., quizzes, checklists)

(continued on page 86)

Exercise 5-1. Are you ready to facilitate a learning event (continued)?

Structured Exercises

_____ Solo work

_____ Guided discussion/question-and-answer session

_____ Small group discussion

_____ Group inquiry

_____ Information search

_____ Small group assignment/problem solving

_____ Peer teaching

_____ Games

_____ Debrief

2. List each of the skill practice activities in the left column of the following chart. For each skill practice, indicate if it is psychomotor, intellectual, or interpersonal by placing an X in the appropriate box.
Then, indicate if there is alignment of the type of skill practice learning activity with the type of skill
by placing a Y (yes) or N (no) in the corresponding column.

Skill Practice	Psychomotor Skill	Intellectual Skill	Interpersonal Skill	Y	N

3. Indicate which of the following transfer activities are built into the course by putting an X in the
space next to it:

_____ Action performance contracting

_____ Application discussion

_____ Barriers and strategies

_____ Enablers and strategies

_____ Structured note taking

_____ Inviting managers to be on a panel that hears participants' presentations and makes comments
on their job relevance

_____ Case studies

_____ Team projects

_____ Letters

4. List the course learning objectives in the left column. List the learning activity(ies) that corresponds with the learning objective in the next column. Indicate if there is alignment between the learning objectives and learning activities by placing a Y (yes) or N (no) in the corresponding column.

Learning Objective	Learning Activity(ies)	Y	N

5. Are at least two out of the three learning styles preferences (visual, auditory, kinesthetic) accommodated in every activity?

Yes_____ No_____

Now that you've had a chance to explore facilitation of specific learning activities and facilitation strategies that support different types of activities, the next chapter will address universal techniques that can be used to gain engagement and participation.

6

Facilitation Techniques

▪▪▪▪▪▪▪▪▪▪▪▪▪▪▪▪▪▪▪▪▪▪▪▪▪▪▪▪▪▪▪▪▪▪▪▪▪▪▪

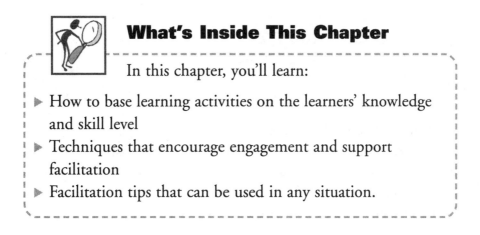

What's Inside This Chapter

In this chapter, you'll learn:

▶ How to base learning activities on the learners' knowledge and skill level
▶ Techniques that encourage engagement and support facilitation
▶ Facilitation tips that can be used in any situation.

Being a facilitator means making sure all important points are brought out, giving everyone a chance to contribute and participate, and checking that everything is going well for the participants. *In other words, being a facilitator means making learning happen.* It also means that you don't have to be the one doing all of the talking—as a matter of fact, the more you create opportunity for the participants to do the talking, the more they will make your points for you, and the more engaged they will be. There are multiple considerations that will guide you into facilitating at the appropriate level of engagement.

How Much Do the Learners Already Know?

The choice of type of learning activity must depend on the level of knowledge and skills that the learners already possess. This is a main area you should focus on when you check the learning objectives and the activities in the course design. It is also a major piece of information you should glean from the audience profile.

Sometimes the information you gather about the learners indicates that you must adjust a learning activity to meet the knowledge or skill level of your learners. A good guideline is that learners should have the first crack at the learning so that the learning activity chosen engages them at the highest level they can manage. That's why facilitators use structured discovery exercises at the beginning of a course or lesson for experienced learners: Because the learners know something of the content, they are able to generate some content themselves, and the facilitator confirms and builds on that knowledge.

Basic Rule 22
Know the knowledge and experience levels of your audience.

Critical Facilitation Factors
Engaging Participants in Content/Knowledge/Comprehension Activities

Because learners are relatively passive during this type of activity, it is important to engage them as much as possible in other ways. Table 6-1 lists some methods that will engage learners during a content/knowledge/comprehension activity.

Sequencing Activities

There is more to sequence than just the flow. Your sequence of activities should vary in pace, intensity, and level of learner involvement. This variation is useful not only in meeting the needs of varied learning styles, but also in helping the learners pace themselves so that they can rest a bit during less intense activities. For example, it would *not* be advisable to have the following lesson sequence:

1. Role play
2. Structured exercise
3. Application activity
4. Debrief discussion.

Table 6-1. Eight ways to engage learners.

1.	Begin with a story, anecdote, statistic, or analogy to hook the learners.
2.	Use visuals and graphics that are colorful and eye-catching.
3.	Separate content into "nice to know" and "need to know."
4.	Present content in small chunks for easy digestion—short lectures and bulleted materials.
5.	Use short content/knowledge/comprehension segments: no more than a 15–20 minute segment before launching learners into something more active.
6.	Take a poll ("How many of you think A? How many of you think B?"): This activity gets learners involved and gives you an idea of where they are in relation to your content.
7.	Change your stance and position in the room; you should be physically active.
8.	Use a bulleted flipchart, overhead, or slide, and uncover each point as it is being discussed.

Reprinted with permission from Deb Tobey LLC, 2003.

You and the learners would be exhausted! A better example of sequence would be the following:

1. Lecture
2. Structured exercise
3. Discussion
4. Application
5. Debrief discussion.

The lecture and discussion provide rest stops between more intense activities. As this example demonstrates, there are several sequencing decisions that must be made. One decision involves building interest with easy content first, followed by more demanding content. A second sequencing decision involves mastering each subskill all the way through the skill practices before putting them together in a comprehensive skill practice. Another decision is always to have a debrief discussion when an activity is over: It solidifies the content for the learners and provides another rest stop in the lesson sequence.

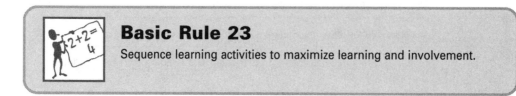

Basic Rule 23
Sequence learning activities to maximize learning and involvement.

Providing Instructions

For structured exercises and skill practices, you need to give the learners explicit instructions for the activity. Although you might present the instructions verbally at the start, the instructions must also be visible at all times during the activity on a flipchart, slide, or handout so that learners can refer back to them. You don't want your activity to be derailed by the learners constantly asking, "Now what is it we are supposed to do?"

The instructions must also be as specific as possible, telling the learners what they are to do in step-by-step fashion; you can even number each step or requirement for clarity. Your instructions should also explain the purpose behind the activity. Some learners are unwilling to participate unless they understand how the activity will be useful. Figure 6-1 offers an example of activity instructions that could be presented on a handout, flipchart, overhead transparency, or PowerPoint slide.

Basic Rule 24
Present complete instructions for all learning activities.

Structuring Time

Your facilitator's guide should have approximate times listed for activities. You'll want to always keep that time in mind during facilitation and also be prepared to adjust the time according to the learning progress.

Figure 6-1. Example of activity instructions for the learners.

Small Group Activity Instructions: "What would you do if...?"

Purpose:
1. To apply your knowledge of traffic signs and signals by planning your actions in various situations you will encounter.
2. Prepare you for the actual driving situations you will encounter.
3. Provide an opportunity for you to share your ideas.

How:
1. Form small groups of three or four.
2. Read and discuss the driving/traffic scenarios on the handout.
3. For each scenario, devise a plan of action.
4. Choose a reporter to present your group's work.
5. Be ready to present in 20 minutes

Basic Rule 25
Manage your time to maximize learning.

Generally speaking, the most time in a lesson should be devoted to skill practice. When you adjust time, the adjustment must *not* be to take a significant amount of time out of the skill practice portion. This is when participants practice and apply, helping to ensure learning and transfer.

Basic Rule 26
Don't sacrifice skill practice when making time adjustments.

Deciding on Group Size

Group size varies: individual, pairs, trios, small groups, large groups, entire group. There are two factors to consider in deciding on group size: what learners will do in the activity and where you are in the course.

The complexity of the task the learners have to accomplish may dictate a certain group size. Think through exactly what they will do and how they will do it, and decide on group size accordingly. Generally speaking, the more complex the task (lots of steps, lots of movement, higher difficulty), the smaller the group. Yet, you don't want the group to be so small that sharing and interaction don't occur. Your facilitator guide suggests an appropriate group size, but you need to use your knowledge of the audience profile and the schedule to make a real-time decision.

Generally, small groups should be used early in the course and larger groups later on. When the learners don't know each other yet, it is less threatening to interact in a pair or trio. Later, when the learners know each other better, they are more comfortable speaking and participating in larger groups. This dynamic is especially important if there are many reserved or shy people in the course.

Basic Rule 27
Align group sizes with the learning activity and course schedule.

Grouping the Learners

The method used to form groups has a greater effect than it first appears. Three main principles support grouping decisions:

1. Form different size groups at different times to adjust to the type of activity and for variety's sake.
2. Participants who are more reserved generally open up in smaller groups.
3. The more challenging, controversial, or uncomfortable the material, the smaller the groups should be.

Think About This

Each time you form groups, mix the learners up so they are not with the same people each time. That way, you increase openness among the learners and reduce any discomfort they may have. Also, each participant will be exposed to the expertise and views of more group members.

Think About This

Counting off for random groupings can be made more fun by using words to count off rather than numbers. For example, if you need four groups, you can count off by the "Beatles" method—John, Paul, George, Ringo. The groups will then have an identity that you can continue to use: "Okay, 'George', what did you discover in your discussion?" Other ideas include using the "Three Stooges" method to make three groups (Larry, Moe, Curly) or the "Rocky and Bullwinkle" method to make two groups. Use a method that fits your style and imagination!

Random Grouping. To group learners randomly, simply have the learners count off by the number of groups you need. That is, have them count off "1, 2, 3, 4" if you need to have four groups.

Learner Choice Grouping. This method gives the learners a choice and allows them to join a group according to their interests in the subject. As long as your groups come out fairly even in number, the activity will work.

Experience Level Grouping. Have the learners mix up according to experience so that each group has at least one member who is experienced in the subject matter who can act as an informal coach. This method spreads out the experience so less experienced learners can be with someone who has "been there, done that." It is also a good technique to use to engage experienced learners at a time when the material may be a little too easy for them.

Assessment Tool Grouping. If you are using an individual assessment tool (leadership style, for example), there might be a time when you want learners who have similar outcomes to work together. In this example, you would put all the learners of one leadership style together in one group. If you do that, be prepared to join and help a group that happens to have significantly less members than the other groups.

Transfer Strategy Grouping. In some cases, you can set up teams by grouping together those who have similar performance contract requirements or similar action

Think About This

Don't try grouping learners according to assessment tool outcomes if what has been assessed is skills or knowledge. Putting learners together because they are at the same skill or knowledge level does not tend to benefit learning, and it has a tendency to stigmatize.

plan strategies and tasks. This strategy allows participants to discuss job application issues they have in common.

Seating Arrangement Grouping. In some cases, you may have a setup that restricts movement of participants. An example is the pit-style, fixed table and chair arrangements. In a situation like this, you can group participants by having them swivel their chairs and work with those behind them.

Noted

It's a bad idea to group learners according to a characteristic that is not learning related (for example, grouping by sex, age, race, and so forth). Facilitators sometimes make the mistake of doing this because they think the characteristic/category they have chosen will generate results that are illustrative; for example, if the male groups all say one thing and the female groups all say another thing, that will demonstrate a content point about sex differences. This practice is based on stereotyping and insulting to the participants. Your learning opportunity will be lost because not everyone who shares one characteristic agrees with each other in other areas as well. In the sex difference example, putting men and women in the same group and then having each group report on the differences observed in their group is much more interactive and supportive of learning.

Monitoring Activities

In structured exercises and skill practices, you let the learners work on their own. This is not the time to step out for a drink of water or to make a quick phone call!

Basic Rule 28

Develop group composition that maximizes attainment of learning objectives and reinforces learning.

You must remain in the room, be available for questions and coaching, and circulate to make sure the groups are working effectively. Typical items that you must attend to while monitoring:

▶ *Reiterating or explaining the activity instructions:* Although keeping instructions visible during the exercise helps in this area, some learners will inevitably ask "Now what are we supposed to do, again?"

▶ *Providing assistance if learners are stuck:* If you discover that a group of learners is truly stumped as to how to accomplish the task you've assigned, you can stop by the group and assist by asking targeted questions to help get the learners on the right track. Very rarely should you just tell them the solution, but subtle assistance is appropriate at times.

▶ *Doing a time check:* Assess whether the learners need more or less time to complete the task. If they appear to be working hard and the original time limit is up, you can announce that they have extra time. If they are finished and are sidetracking into conversations, say, "I can see that everyone is finished; let's come back together and see what you came up with." If one group finishes early and is sidetracking, you can add an additional task, taking them into more depth or application to the job.

▶ *Listening in on discussions:* You want to find out what the learners' hot topics are in their work together, what ideas they had, and pick up on their issues and concerns. When you conduct the debrief discussion, you'll be able to speak their language.

▶ *Giving time warnings:* Let the groups know when their time is almost up so they can wrap up their discussions and not feel interrupted.

Basic Rule 29

Continue in your role of facilitator by monitoring while participants are engaged in activities.

Feedback for the Learners

Facilitators have many opportunities to provide feedback to the learners. An obvious opportunity is during a guided discussion in which you ask a pre-planned question to the group, the learners respond, and you follow up with additional information that augments the comments. When an individual responds, you want to affirm him or her and, if you can, the response. You can say such things as, "That's good" or "Great response" or "I like that, anyone else have a comment?"

Other times, the respondent may provide a superficial answer and you want more depth. In this case, you can say something such as, "Yes, now can you tell me more?" or "OK, now take me deeper into what you have in mind" or "Great start, what else can we say about that?" While you are affirming, you are also letting the learners know that there is more learning to be gained from the question.

A more difficult situation is when the learner's response is incorrect; then, you cannot afford to agree. Some facilitators agree with comments that are wrong in order to avoid confronting the issue or to be supportive of the learner. This tactic is not recommended. Part of giving feedback is to indicate when a learner gives an incorrect response. Yes, you still want to affirm the learner, but not the incorrect answers. In this case, say something like, "I understand what you are saying, however that relates more to . . ." or you can paraphrase the response and indicate that this relates more to something else than to the current subject. You can also use the tactic of responding by saying, "Let me reframe the question" and ask the question in another way. By all means, be tactful, but do not accept answers that are wrong, incomplete, or superficial. Your role is to ensure that a complete response is provided by the group.

Tests and Assessments

Tests and assessments—whether written or oral—also provide feedback to participants. Test question formats must align with the learning objectives. For example, if your learning objective says the participants "will be able to recognize (certain items)," your test can contain a matching or multiple-choice question. If the learning objective indicates that the participants "will be able to list (certain items)," the test questions can ask the participants to list the items, put a list in order, or match items with their definitions.

The purpose of these types of tests is to assess knowledge and provide immediate feedback to the learners. Because these are used for development, an important

Basic Rule 30

The type of test or assessment must align with the learning objectives.

step is for you to go over the tests and rationale for missed questions. This not only gives feedback, but also reinforces content.

What about testing skills or behaviors and providing feedback? In this case you should have a checklist that is used in conjunction with a learning activity. For example, if the participants are to demonstrate a procedure, you have a behavioral observation checklist of those steps, and learners will use the checklist to observe each other. Intellectual skills are generally assessed by how well a person solves a problem situation or case study. If they are to demonstrate an intellectual skill (for example, "plan a car trip using a map"), you have a quality checklist that lists criteria for "what a good car trip plan looks like," and that checklist will be used to evaluate the quality of the plan. The checklist can be a scaled instrument (0–4, with descriptors for each rating) to assess the quality of the case solution. You have the correct case solution that you then match to the solution provided by the learners. In assessing the learner's case solution, you are looking for completeness and quality of content.

Interpersonal skills are usually assessed in a behavior modeling or role-play assessment. Say, for example, that the behavior being assessed is "conducting a coaching conversation." To assess this skill, you'll use a checklist of the steps and skills associated with each step of a coaching session to observe a learner practicing the skill of conducting a coaching conversation. If you are assessing the skill for step-by-step behaviors only, the checklist will contain the process steps for a coaching conversation in order with a yes/no answer, so the observer can indicate that the learner did or did not follow the process. However, you might also be assessing the coaching conversation skill for quality. In that case, the checklist will contain criteria regarding how well (quality statements) participants demonstrated the process steps rather than simply a yes/no answer as to whether they demonstrated the step. The observer then completes the checklist and provides objective feedback to the learner.

Although your facilitator's guide provides instructions, there are usually a couple of options here for how to structure the activity. For example, in the coaching session role-play example, if other learners provide peer feedback, you can form learner triads with one learner using the checklist to observe and give feedback to the one practicing the skill; then triad members exchange roles. This setup ensures complete feedback. If you use a fishbowl technique, wherein a few learners enact the role-play and are observed by the rest of the group, you provide the feedback yourself. In either case, there is a document of objective feedback based on the skills/behaviors observed.

Think About This

Tests and assessments provide objective feedback to the learners. The instruments are built into the learning activity and should allow for practice or application and reinforce content. The more objective and comprehensive the instrument, the better the feedback is.

Debriefing Sessions

Debriefing sessions are great opportunities to provide feedback to learners, both during learning activities and especially after the activity is complete. As learners make their presentations, you and the learners are interacting with the presenting group. Here, you are giving feedback in the form of questions, examples, dialogue, and so forth. Or, you have just completed a learning activity, and you now have the opportunity to provide feedback. The debriefing is the time for you to summarize the lessons learned, to reinforce the content, and support transfer. Although the content of the debriefing is in the leader's guide, you want to make real-time comments and applications.

Performance Contracts As Feedback

As you may recall, the learner fills out the performance contract prior to coming to the workshop. It is completed between the individual and his or her manager. This document then becomes a pre-course organizer and document for transfer. It also provides an opportunity to provide feedback to learners. At designated times during the learning event, the participants have the opportunity to apply content through completion or revision of their performance contract. As they complete their work, you engage in a dialogue with them (individually or by group) about some of their ideas and strategies. This feedback helps them to rethink their transfer strategies from a content and job environment perspective.

Basic Rule 31

Feedback, tests, and assessments can be part of learning activities.

Action Planning

Whether done intermittently throughout the learning or at the end, action plans should not be a learner activity only; they also provide an opportunity to provide feedback on course content and transfer. While learners are completing their structured action plans, you can be moving about the room, offering coaching. At the

Noted

Providing objective feedback is critical to learning. When the feedback is in the form of tests and assessments, there is always a question as to who sees the information and how it will be used. It is recommended that you emphasize to your clients (often the managers of your learners) that the feedback is for development and to reinforce learning. After the feedback instrument and process have been completed in the course, it is suggested that you do not collect the information unless it is for facilitator development (more on this in chapter 9). Even then, collect this information only in aggregate, anonymous form. In some cases, managers may want to see individuals' performance. Resist such requests. You never know how that information may be used. There are legal ramifications if this information is used for HR types of decisions (merit, promotion, demotion, termination, and so forth). Maintain a learner privacy position.

Think About This

Given the great value in learners' discovering new knowledge rather than just being "told," one of the best learning moments a facilitator can create is "the personal aha." A personal aha occurs when the learner realizes that what he or she has been doing up until this point is incorrect and then discovers the right way to do it. And, this realization happens in a way that does not embarrass the learner; the aha is personal and private. For example, in a course for managers on how to conduct job interviews, one of the learning activities might be to watch a video of someone conducting a job interview incorrectly. The group then critiques what they saw. For those learners who have been conducting interviews incorrectly, this activity helps them discover and correct their mistakes in an individual, personal, and nonpublic way.

conclusion of the planning or that segment of the planning, learners can share their plans. As a facilitator of learning, you can then reinforce the content, add ideas for transfer, and involve the larger group in a dialogue about ideas.

Adjusting on the Fly

The mark of an excellent learning facilitator is the ability to adjust "on the fly" to changing conditions without shortchanging the learning process. The most common causes for adjusting on the fly are

- an unexpected change in time constraints (fire drill, a productive tangent, a surprise guest speaker, learners working faster or slower than you expected, a late start for the course)
- a prior assumption or assessment about the learners is off target (they are more or less experienced than you thought; their backgrounds are not what you thought they were; they are more or less open to certain types of activities than you expected).

Given the main causes for adjusting (time and learner characteristics), three main adjustment factors are available to you: learner groupings, logistics of the activity, and activity intensity. The actual adjustments you make involve either increasing or decreasing the parameters of the activity in one or more of these three areas.

Learner Groupings

The original plan for grouping learners in an activity is based on the grouping arrangement that will support the greatest amount of learning within the planned time. When reality gets in the way of your plan, a facilitator can adjust on the fly the number of learner groups working together, which changes the sizes of the individual groups. The guiding principle is this: The more learner groups, the more time and involvement the activity will take.

A couple of examples will clarify the use of this strategy. If you are running short on time, decrease the number of groupings for an activity in which you had planned for the learners to work in pairs or trios. Instead, have them work in groups of five or six. This way, there will be fewer groups to report on their work, and the overall activity will take less time. Conversely, increase the number of groups by breaking down larger groups into pairs or trios if more time has become available.

Or, consider the situation when you find that the planned groupings require more or less involvement than the learners are comfortable with. You'll have to increase or decrease the number of groupings in this case as well. For example, if you have more shy learners than you expected, you may need to increase the number of groups to more, but smaller, groups. If learners are more comfortable in large groups and seem to enjoy speaking in front of others, then decreasing the number to a few larger groups (or one large group) may be appropriate.

Logistics of the Activity

Activity logistics can be adjusted for time or for changing learner needs. When you plan the logistics of an activity ahead of time, it is much easier to adjust on the fly when necessary. Logistics issues include the number of groups; physical layout of the room; conditions in which the learners will work (Will they discuss? Work alone, then discuss? Move around? Stay in the same place?); results they must produce (report out, flipchart, presentation, action); time of day (need to be more physically active later in the day); and learning styles (is there a preponderance of one style?).

What it comes down to is this: The more active or complicated the logistics, the more time and active learner involvement the activity will take.

If you've run short on time, a logistics adjustment you can make is decreasing the complexity of the logistics. For example, have learners appoint a recorder to take notes in their group, rather than have them draw up a flipchart. Or, have groups report their top three ideas rather than all of the ideas they discussed.

Conversely, if more time is available, you can increase the complexity of your logistics. For example, have groups do something physically active, like build a model, solve a puzzle, or make a flipchart. Or, have them work on assignments in segments and switch groups between segments. Alternatively, instead of having each group provide a complete report, you can use a round robin. In this situation, each group presents an idea. The next group adds a different one. This goes on until all ideas have been presented. This method reduces the amount of redundancy on reports.

If you find that the planned logistics will support more or less active involvement than is optimal with a particular group of learners, you can adjust the logistics accordingly. You can decrease the logistics for learners who are shy, reserved, novices, sedentary, or at the beginning of a course when they don't know each other; and you can increase the logistics for learners who are more extroverted, outgoing, experienced, active in their jobs, and later in a course when comfort levels are higher.

Activity Intensity

Activity intensity can also be adjusted to accommodate time issues or learner needs. The more learner centered an activity is, the more intense an experience it is for the learners. Intensity of activities ranges from lectures (low intensity) to discussions (moderately low intensity) to structured exercises (moderate intensity) to skill practices (high intensity). Here's a guideline: The more intense the activity, the more time it will take and the more risk learners experience.

For example, if you have run short on time, you can decrease the activity intensity one step (adjust a skill practice on the content to a structured exercise; adjust a structured exercise to a discussion; adjust a discussion to a lecture). If time is available, you will keep the activity at the planned level of intensity (no need to increase or decrease intensity).

You may find yourself in the situation in which the planned activity's intensity is not a good match for the learners' comfort zone or experience level. Once again,

Noted

When the intensity of an activity is decreased, the depth of the learning will also be decreased. For that reason, you may have to make later adjustments in your skill practices and measurement/assessment activities.

you can adjust on the fly. You can decrease the intensity (from a skill practice on the content to a structured exercise; from a structured exercise to a discussion; from a discussion to a lecture). You can also increase intensity with learners who are beyond the planned intensity in either their comfort zone or experience (increase intensity from a lecture to a discussion, from a discussion to a structured exercise, from a structured exercise to a skill practice).

The most important aspect of adjusting on the fly is preparing ahead of time. Know which content and activities are most critical and which are nice to know. Know which activities reinforce skills and link to application to the job. Analyze your content and activities and identify what you will adjust if necessary and how you will adjust it. Develop ahead of time the specific changes you will make in groupings, logistics, or activity intensity should the need arise. In the classroom, when you make the actual adjustment, it will be seamless in the eyes of your learners—and that's what counts!

Basic Rule 32

Plan ahead to adjust on the fly to maintain content and make learning happen.

Facilitation Tips

You may be asking right about now, "What about when I am actually in front of the group? What do I do then?" You already know part of the answer because it lies in your own presentation skills. In addition, chapter 4 offered you some advice about facilitating. Now, table 6-2 provides additional tips to get you going.

Table 6-2. Facilitation tips.

Tip	Explanation
Ask questions to gain participation.	Ask open-ended questions that invite response, especially "what" and "how" questions. Close-ended questions stifle participation. Use closed-ended questions only when you want to end discussion and move on.
Use transitions.	Learners need to know when one topic has closed and another has begun. Transitions don't have to be fancy. A statement as simple as "Now that we have discussed A, let's move on to B" works well.
Control discussions.	Regardless of the participation level, you are still in charge. You can choose to move on when it's appropriate by saying something like, "OK, one more comment and then we have to move on." If the discussion becomes repetitive, take control and make a transition to the next subject.
Remain neutral.	If the group gets into a debate about a particular point, clarify and summarize both sides, and then move on. Don't express your own opinion (unless the debate concerns a factual matter) because the participants who have the opposite opinion may feel put down.
Don't wing it.	Winging it carries some very big risks; you might go on time-consuming tangents, you might lead yourself into a discussion that is not appropriate, or you might steal your own thunder for a later subject.
Affirm.	Find something to reinforce and affirm in every comment. You can always affirm a person's effort at participation. When you treat people with respect, they will feel comfortable participating.
Watch and respond to body language.	Say, "Joe, you look puzzled. Is something not making sense?"
Don't be afraid of silence.	Sometimes people are simply thinking and need a little time. When you ask a question, mentally count to 10 (slowly!) before asking again or redirecting the question.
Debrief thoroughly.	Plan key questions that you will ask at the end of an activity or exercise to be sure that the participants get all of the important points. Don't ad lib a debriefing session! Highlight the lessons learned for each activity.

Reprinted with permission from Deb Tobey LLC, 2003.

Getting It Done

In this chapter you were introduced to a variety of facilitation techniques to enhance learning. Doing your work as a facilitator in the areas of sequencing, activity instructions, timing, group sizes, grouping techniques, monitoring activities, giving feedback, and adjusting on the fly will ensure a complete and effective learning experience for your learners. Exercise 6-1 is another opportunity for you to plan additional skill development for yourself.

Exercise 6-1. Facilitation techniques self-assessment.

Instructions:
1. Assess your confidence level in each of the facilitation areas below by circling the appropriate number.
2. For low areas of confidence, indicate the actions you will take to develop that technique.

Facilitation Technique	Low Confidence	Moderate Confidence	High Confidence	Actions for Development
Assessing learners' current knowledge level	1	2	3	
Engaging learners during a content/knowledge/ comprehension activity	1	2	3	
Sequencing content and activities	1	2	3	
Providing activity instructions	1	2	3	
Allotting and adjusting time	1	2	3	
Choosing and managing group sizes	1	2	3	
Grouping learners optimally	1	2	3	
Monitoring learning activities	1	2	3	
Giving learners feedback	1	2	3	

(continued on page 108)

Exercise 6-1. Facilitation techniques self-assessment (continued).

Facilitation Technique	Low Confidence	Moderate Confidence	High Confidence	Actions for Development
Managing assessments and measurement	1	2	3	
Adjusting on the fly	1	2	3	
Questioning	1	2	3	
Using transitions	1	2	3	
Controlling discussions	1	2	3	
Remaining neutral in debates	1	2	3	
Avoiding winging it	1	2	3	
Affirming	1	2	3	
Watching and responding to body language	1	2	3	
Being comfortable with, and capitalizing on, silence	1	2	3	
Conducting debriefing discussions	1	2	3	

In chapter 7, every facilitator's "favorite" learner is discussed: the difficult participant!

7

Managing Difficult Participants

■ ■

What's Inside This Chapter

In this chapter, you'll learn:

▶ Why facilitators label some learners as difficult
▶ How to stop labeling people and start labeling behavior
▶ About the thought process that drives facilitator reactions to disruptive learner behavior
▶ About choosing to act on a professional agenda rather than on a personal agenda
▶ Specific facilitator techniques that manage disruptive behaviors without disrupting the learning.

It Takes All Kinds of Learners

You can expect several types of learners in any learning environment. First, there are the people who want to learn and who are there voluntarily. Yet, they have their own idiosyncrasies that can unintentionally get in the way of the learning. Next, some folks want to hone a skill or pick up new ideas. Even though they are present because they want to be, they also have their own idiosyncrasies and knowledge/skill/expertise that can unintentionally get in the way of the learning. Then there are the people who have been sent to your course by their managers. They have to be there, but they don't want to be. Even though their bodies are in the seats, their minds were "checked at the door." These folks, though, will do everything possible to intentionally disrupt the learning. Finally, some people will be in your course because they are taking a break from the daily grind. They really don't care one way or the other about the learning, and their lack of involvement can disrupt the learning.

Regardless of which group a participant might belong to, all these groups have some things in common:

- ▶ They are trying to fulfill their individual needs and agendas, which may or may not be related to the learning experience at any given moment.
- ▶ Their individual agendas drive their own (and sometimes the group's) behavior that can disrupt the learning.
- ▶ Facilitators tend to label these folks as difficult participants.

A Clash of Agendas

Why do some people end up labeled as difficult participants? Say that a participant challenges your expertise in front of the class because of his or her personal agenda of wanting to be acknowledged for his or her expertise. This behavior is not directed at you, and it's not about you—but it feels like it is!

It's very easy for you to react personally, and a personal agenda arises on your part, which might be to prove your own expertise and avoid damaging (or possibly even enhancing) your own credibility in front of the class. So, a behavior arises out of your own personal agenda, and you get into a debate with the participant. Who wins? No one!

This behavior on the facilitator's part disrupts the learning process just as much as the participant's original behavior does! One of you (if not both) will lose face, the class is disrupted, the participant involved is now an "enemy" and will probably accelerate his or her behavior or work behind the scenes to discredit you, the rest of the group is excluded from the learning experience, and you've lost credibility as a facilitator because the rest of the group hesitates to continue to participate because of fear of getting into a similar debate when they express their opinions.

In short, learning ceases because the facilitator has taken the participant's disruptive behavior personally and has acted on that reaction.

No way, you say: "I don't take their behavior personally! That's not me!" An observer would beg to differ, starting with the label of difficult participant. Labeling others as difficult is as personal as it gets! And, by the way, think about who they are making it difficult for. Not for themselves: They are making it difficult for you and other participants! If you think that this person is difficult and that you have to make him or her stop being that way, you are much more likely to personalize your responses to difficult behavior. When you personalize your response (getting drawn into a debate, for example), the situation becomes "about you," rather than about the learning.

Basic Rule 33

Learners behave in a way that disrupts learning to fulfill an individual need or agenda.

A Closer Look

To make matters worse, all this turmoil happens so quickly in your mind that you're not even aware it's going on! To make sense of this situation, you must slow it down and recognize that what's happening is a complex thought process with several steps, beginning with the learner's behavior and ending with your behavior.

Let's take a "slow-motion" look at the example, breaking down the process into steps:

1. Learner behavior occurs: *challenges facilitator's expertise.*
2. Facilitator thinks, *"This learner is being difficult by challenging my expertise."*
3. Facilitator thinks, *"I've got to save (or, I hope, enhance) my expertise and credibility in front of the group. I can't let this learner embarrass me."*
4. Facilitator thinks, *"I'll show him or her that I'm right,"* and launches into a debate with the learner.
5. The situation (in this case a debate) escalates: *The facilitator must now prove he or she is right, or credibility is lost. The learner must prove he or she is right, or humiliation will occur.*

6. The rest of the learners become disengaged, even embarrassed at having to witness the exchange.

7. Result: *The learning is disrupted, and the facilitator has lost credibility (the main thing the facilitator was trying to avoid).*

A Better Way

A facilitator's response to difficult behavior must be depersonalized. The depersonalizing process begins by making a change in how difficult participants are considered. Rather than label *them* difficult participants, call *it* disruptive behavior. In this way, you are labeling behavior—not people—which is a good place to start depersonalizing the event. Also, the term *disruptive* is both less personal and more accurate in describing the effects of that behavior.

Think About This

Right now, go back to the title of this chapter, cross it out, and change it to "Facilitating Disruptive Behavior."

In dealing with disruptive behavior, your job is to set aside your personal agendas and concentrate on fulfilling your professional agenda, which is, without fail, to make the learning happen. This agenda is true no matter what the situation, but it is particularly important when in the presence of disruptive behavior. Your actions must focus always on helping the learning to occur.

Figure 7-1 illustrates what must happen in a facilitator's thought processes when disruptive behavior occurs.

Noted

When a facilitator's expertise is challenged by a learner, the wrong answer is "Well, I have a Ph.D. in this area," or "Well, you know I have 20 years' experience in this line of work." These responses don't hold water with learners in terms of establishing credibility! As adult learners, they are already challenging your credibility by saying that your information is not in sync with their experiences and background. The only way to handle this situation is to facilitate discussion regarding what their experiences are and how your information fits them.

Figure 7-1. Recognizing and responding to disruptive learner behavior: understanding the thought process.

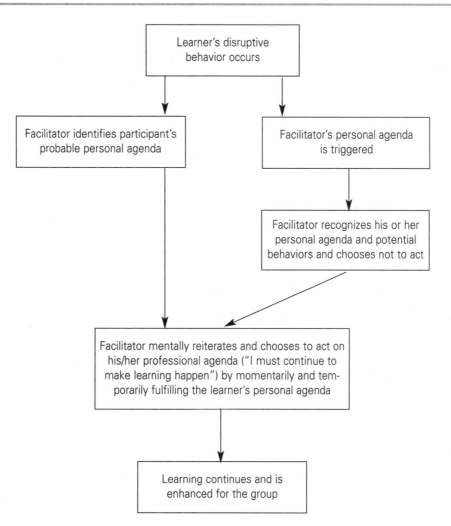

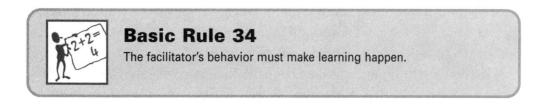

Basic Rule 34

The facilitator's behavior must make learning happen.

Noted

To enhance and make learning happen, the facilitator does not embarrass the learner who is behaving in a disruptive manner. Creating embarrassment or discomfort for that learner goes beyond extinguishing the person's behavior and makes it personal. Not only is that learner's experience ruined, but the learning is disrupted for the other learners as well. If the behavior is so disruptive that it must be dealt with individually, take it outside the learning environment and talk with the learner privately.

Believe it or not (and, frankly, like it or not), acting on the professional agenda of making learning happen often means helping the participant in question meet his or her personal agenda—*momentarily and temporarily.* If you have successfully depersonalized the situation, those things won't matter nearly as much as your desire to continue the learning.

When a facilitator acts on a personal agenda, it gets in the way of the learning for everyone—not just for the disruptive participant. So the effective facilitator chooses not to acknowledge or act on personal agendas. Is this easy to do? Not always. It means focusing your efforts on the learning process and letting go of personal needs that might crop up in response to the disruptive behavior. It means doing whatever it takes to support and continue the learning process—even if it means giving in to a specific participant and letting him or her have what he or she wants even when you personally don't want to do so.

More often than not, once you meet that person's agenda, the agenda goes away, and the disruptive behavior is extinguished. So, in the example here, the participant's agenda is "wanting to be acknowledged for his expertise." If your only agenda is "make the learning happen," you can see that by allowing a few minutes for this person to pontificate, his agenda is fulfilled, the disruptive behavior stops, the group has probably learned something new from this participant's expertise, and everyone can get on with the learning. What you will have done in this case is chosen a facilitator behavior that focuses on the learning, not on yourself.

Does learner disruptive behavior extinguish itself once you have met the learner's agenda every time? No. Sometimes allowing a learner to take the spotlight and pontificate (as in the example) can result in that person's behavior becoming even more disruptive by wanting to be the expert in many discussion points. He or she can then tend to monopolize the class discussion. If this happens, a new disruptive behavior is recognized and must be managed.

Think About This

What do you do if the learner has done something extremely inappropriate, such as making a racist remark? Does the rule about not embarrassing learners apply in this situation as well? Obviously, the behavior must be extinguished—and quickly. And, if you deal with the learner privately (so as not to embarrass him or her), you run the risk of the other learners' not knowing that you handled the situation and thus assuming that you think the behavior was acceptable. Try first behaving as if the learner is unaware of the impact of the remark ("We know you didn't mean that the way it sounded"), thereby giving the learner the opportunity to recant the remark. If he or she does not recant, then you must immediately say something that lets the offending learner and the other learners know that the remark is unacceptable: "As you know, this organization does not share that view, and we can't give the impression that it's OK to say that."

Does this approach mean that your personal agendas go away, that your personal need for credibility as a facilitator isn't important, that your opinion that a participant truly is difficult isn't valid? No, your agendas and opinions are just as valid as anyone else's; you just can't act on them in the learning moment. The moment you act on a personal agenda, the course becomes about you, not about the learning, and not about the participants. As one consultant says, "You can have your personal agenda after 6:00," meaning that facilitators must vent and express personal agendas outside of the learning environment and only with trusted colleagues.

Making a Judgment Call

What happens if you take all the recommended steps for shutting down disruptive behavior but it still continues? At that point, you have a dilemma. The science of group dynamics has shown that when disruptive behavior is allowed to continue, the group sometimes will eventually shut down that behavior for themselves. Some of the things they will do in this regard include shunning the participant who is behaving disruptively, negative nonverbal behaviors (eye-rolling, for example), ignoring

Think About This

An interesting facet of group dynamics is that once disruptive behavior shuts down, the group refocuses on you rather than on the participant who was being disruptive. So, when you do something that acts on a personal agenda and preemptively shut down a participant in a disruptive way, the rest of the group will shut down as well out of fear that you might do the same thing to them. They, in effect, turn on you, and this will happen *even if the group is happy that you have shut the person down.* Shutting someone down in a negative way can be momentarily satisfying for both you and the learner group, but it's not worth it in the long run—no matter how much the person seems to deserve it.

and not responding to the participant's remarks, and carrying on side conversations when that participant is speaking. That is a more desirable scenario than you having to continue to deal with the behavior or having to shut it down yourself, but it doesn't always happen this way.

So, do you wait and hope the group will become so frustrated with that behavior that they shut the person down? Do you continue to act on your professional agenda in dealing with the behavior and hope that the third time is the charm? Do you take the matter into your own hands and deal with the person in a more disciplinary manner?

It's your call. There will be times when your judgment is called into play, when you believe you must act more leniently than you'd like, or more firmly than you'd like. As another colleague says, "Once you know the rules, you know when to break them." That is your judgment call. Sooner or later, you will experience the Catch-22 of facilitation: If you err on the side of leniency, you will receive negative evaluations that say you are "too nice." If you err on the side of firmness, you will receive negative evaluations that say you are "too strict." Although your desire is to always have your facilitation be "just right," sometimes it just comes down to a judgment call.

Table 7-1 presents and dissects many of the disruptive situations that you might experience. Features include

- ▶ identification of participant behaviors that facilitators tend to think are disruptive to learning

- typical facilitator personal agendas that can occur in each disruptive situation and the responsive behaviors that should *not* be used (even though it is tempting to do so)
- typical participant agendas that drive disruptive behaviors
- a reminder that your professional agenda is *always* to enhance and make learning happen
- a range of facilitator responses that can fulfill your professional agenda and are most likely to allow learning to continue, as well as a reminder that often the most effective facilitator behavior involves fulfilling the participant's personal agenda—momentarily and temporarily.

Noted

Why include information about facilitators' personal agendas and inappropriate facilitator responses? Many times facilitators can be unaware of the personal reaction and agenda that may occur when disruptive behavior appears and are, therefore, unaware of the behaviors that personal agendas drive. Remember, you are functioning very quickly in a complex internal thought process. So, it's just as important to recognize and reject unacceptable behaviors as it is to own effective behaviors. You just might see yourself in some of the personal agendas and disruptive behaviors!

In general, facilitator tactics for handling disruptive behavior should include

- not getting caught in one-on-one power struggles
- using good-natured humor
- connecting with the participant on a personal level
- broadening the participation of the rest of the group
- protecting participants as needed
- using a separate issues chart or a "parking lot" to postpone issues until they are appropriate for discussion
- recognizing the learner's point and then taking the discussion offline during breaks, lunches, at the end of the day
- changing the small group composition
- modifying activities or instructional strategies.

Table 7-1. Dealing with disruptive behavior.

Learner's disruptive behavior	Facilitator's personal agenda is triggered	Facilitator recognizes his/her personal agenda and potential behaviors and chooses not to act	Facilitator identifies learner's probable personal agenda	Facilitator mentally reiterates professional agenda	Facilitator chooses to act on professional agenda rather than personal agenda. He or she chooses behaviors that meet the learner's agenda and, by doing so, extinguishes disruptive behavior, and continues the learning.
Side conversation	They are being disrespectful and rude. I want to treat them the same way, so they see what it feels like.	"Do you two have something to share?" Ask the class a question, then direct it to one of the disrupters to catch him/her off guard.	Talking about something that is relevant to the class Not engaged in the class; talking to keep themselves involved and/or awake Talking about something that is relevant to work, but not the class	I must continue to make learning happen.	• Behave as if you "know" that the side conversation is class related and ask them to add their thoughts. In the event that the side conversation actually was class related, you have reinforced their involvement and participation. • If you are lecturing or leading a discussion, slowly move into the part of the room where the disrupters are; continue lecture/ discussion and don't look at them as you continue. (This only works if you have already established a habit of moving around the room.) • Change the pace of the activity; do something active (have participants make flipcharts, put them in small group discussions, etc.). • Re-form groups by counting off and make sure the disrupters are separated. • At the start of the next session, revisit the class norms/ground rules.
Talks too much; monopolizes discussion	I am frustrated; I wish this person would shut up—and stay that way.	Anything that shuts the person down in a mean or embarrassing way: joke, labeling him/her as a talker, rolling eyes, etc. Smiling or in some other way colluding with the group if they are rolling eyes, etc.	Wants attention Thinks out loud Wants to demonstrate knowledge/ expertise	I must continue to make learning happen.	• If he/she is on the subject, begin talking with him/her and summarize the point. Then turn to others and invite their participation: "What does everyone else think?" • Avoid eye contact with him/her for a while. • If he/she is off target, say "Great point, but it is beyond the scope of our class . . . Let's talk about this together offline." • Put his/her issue on a "parking lot" flipchart (meaning it is something that will be dealt with at the proper time). • Change the pace of the activity and have participants do solo work for a short time.

Learner's disruptive behavior	Facilitator's personal agenda is triggered	Facilitator recognizes his/her personal agenda and potential behaviors and chooses not to act	Facilitator identifies learner's probable personal agenda	Facilitator mentally reiterates professional agenda	Facilitator chooses to act on professional agenda rather than personal agenda. He or she chooses behaviors that meet the learner's agenda and, by doing so, extinguishes disruptive behavior, and continues the learning.
Complains; is negative about class or organization	What a whiner! This person needs to shut up before he/she brings the whole group down, and I have to somehow bring them back up.	Argue with him/her. Cut him/her off before he/she can finish his/her thought. Say, "Well, there's nothing we can do about that." Refuse to acknowledge the speaker and/or complaint.	Doesn't want to be there Has other things on his/her mind that are more important to him/her Wants complaint to be acknowledged	I must continue to make learning happen.	• Ask if others feel the same way. If they don't, then offer to assist and/or listen to him/her during break. • If others do feel the same way, you might have a productive tangent to deal with (see section about Adjusting on the Fly). Negative feelings and complaints (on the part of the majority of the group) must be acknowledged and handled, or they will simply fester, and learning won't happen. • Acknowledge the complaint, then turn group discussion to strategizing how to overcome it. • Put the issue on the parking lot. • If valid, incorporate it into the action planning to have the learner address the issue.
Daydreams; not "in the class"	This person is being rude to me and is influencing others to drift off. I am embarrassed so I want to embarrass him/her.	Call on him/her unexpectedly. Joke: "Earth to John. Come in, John." Unexpectedly introduce a game/test activity: "Let's see who has been paying attention" (in effect, punishing the whole class).	Not engaged, would rather be somewhere else Content not relevant Just another initiative that will pass	I must continue to make learning happen.	• Change the current activity to make it more active/involving. For example, if they are in small group discussions, have them produce a flipchart showing their work. • If the daydreaming is organization related and more than one person is doing it (for example, everyone's mind is on the current layoff situation), acknowledge it and allow a short discussion, then move on. • Talk to him/her privately during a break and ask how the class could be better meeting his/her needs. • Frequently link content to the job.

(continued on page 120)

Table 7-1. Dealing with disruptive behavior (continued).

Learner's disruptive behavior	Facilitator's personal agenda is triggered	Facilitator recognizes his/her personal agenda and potential behaviors and chooses not to act	Facilitator identifies learner's probable personal agenda	Facilitator mentally reiterates professional agenda	Facilitator chooses to act on professional agenda rather than personal agenda. He or she chooses behaviors that meet the learner's agenda and, by doing so, extinguishes disruptive behavior, and continues the learning.
Heckles the facilitator	Smart aleck! I want to put him/her down like he/she is putting me down.	Continue to "volley" with the heckler as the rest of the group watches. Label the behavior in front of the group: "Oh, so we have a smart aleck in our midst!"	Wants attention Clown: Thinks the heckling is funny, not rude Doesn't want to be there Wants to destroy facilitator's credibility	I must continue to make learning happen.	• Give him/her attention in a learning-oriented way rather than encourage the heckling: "Mary, you clearly have some background in this area; would you share your thoughts with the rest of the group?" • Change the activity so that the participants are interacting with each other rather than you. • If the heckling continues, talk with the person privately: Ask if the class is meeting his/her needs. If not, or if he/she doesn't want to be there, acknowledge and support that within the constraints of the program. If it continues, send him/her back to the job.
Challenges the facilitator on content or technique; "know-it-all"	I am the expert; I am the facilitator; I am right. This person is hurting my credibility and should not be allowed to challenge me.	"That may be true in your experience, but we are not talking about that in here" (i.e., your experience is not relevant). Ignoring the person's comments	Wants to be recognized for own expertise Wants some of the spotlight Wants to destroy facilitator's credibility	I must continue to make learning happen.	• Give the person the spotlight for a few minutes. His/her expertise will add to the learning. (Remember, your credibility comes from your ability as a facilitator as well as from your own expertise.) • Turn the exchange into a discussion by implying that there are multiple points of view and all should be addressed. Ask for other opinions from the rest of the group.

Learner's disruptive behavior	Facilitator's personal agenda is triggered	Facilitator recognizes his/her personal agenda and potential behaviors and chooses not to act	Facilitator identifies probable personal agenda	Facilitator mentally reiterates professional agenda	Facilitator chooses to act on professional agenda rather than personal agenda. He or she chooses behaviors that meet the learner's agenda and, by doing so, extinguishes disruptive behavior, and continues the learning.
Tells jokes or clowns around at inappropriate times	This is funny! Or, this isn't funny!	Support the behavior by laughing, etc., or continuing to "banter." Shut the person down by embarrassing him/her.	Wants attention Is uncomfortable with the subject, so makes jokes to help himself/herself handle it Is bored so wants to liven things up	I must continue to make learning happen.	• Give him/her attention by re-engaging him/her with the content without acknowledging the joking behavior. • If discomfort with the subject is apparent in more group members, then the jokes are intended to relieve tension. Help the group by bringing up the discomfort directly; or put them in small groups so they can discuss more comfortably. • When a joke is funny and at the right time, laugh!
Makes an inappropriate remark (sexist, racist, etc.)	What an idiot/bigot/sexist, etc.! I am angry! I want to embarrass this person! Or, I don't know what to do with this; it's better to do nothing than to make a mistake.	React harshly and/or label the person: "We don't make bigoted remarks in here!" Ignore the remark or pretend it didn't happen (implies to participants that you think it's OK).	Truly unaware of how the remark sounded Is aware of how the remark sounded and is purposely making the remark anyway	I must continue to make learning happen.	• You must deal with it in front of the group; it cannot be ignored. • First, give him/her a chance to retract: "I'm sure you didn't mean that the way it sounded…." If he/she does retract, move on. (If he/she was unaware of the meaning of the remark, he/she will suffer enough embarrassment on his/her own; you don't need to intensify it.) • If the person does not retract, say in front of the group, "Unfortunately, that view is not in keeping with the values of our organization, and we can't have any more of that." You may need to speak with the person during break as well—and even report the behavior to his/her manager if necessary. • Revisit norms/ground rules for respect of others.

(continued on page 122)

121

Table 7-1. Dealing with disruptive behavior (continued).

Learner's disruptive behavior	Facilitator's personal agenda is triggered	Facilitator recognizes his/her personal agenda and potential behaviors and chooses not to act	Facilitator identifies learner's probable personal agenda	Facilitator mentally reiterates professional agenda	Facilitator chooses to act on professional agenda rather than personal agenda. He or she chooses behaviors that meet the learner's agenda and, by doing so, extinguishes disruptive behavior, and continues the learning.
Does other work or reads the newspaper or takes cell phone calls	How dare he ignore me! I am embarrassed. I want to embarrass/ punish him/ her.	Direct an unexpected question/remark to the person to make it obvious that he/she isn't paying attention.	Is not engaged

Feels pressure to be doing other work | I must continue to make learning happen. | • Speak to him/her during a break and point out that his/her behavior leads you to believe the class is not meeting his/her needs. Ask how the class can better serve his/her needs and try to do that.
• Acknowledge the pressure. Negotiate with the participant to appear engaged so that his/her behavior doesn't affect the rest of the group.
• Offer to have him/her attend another session. |
| Silent, doesn't participate verbally | I want this person to participate (whether he/she wants to or not!).

Am I not doing a good job? I MUST engage him/her. | Assume that he/she is shy and it's your job to "bring him/her out."

Create participation opportunities that will force him/her to participate. | Is shy and not comfortable speaking up in front of others

Could very well be participating by listening and thinking, etc. (just not speaking)

Is primarily a "thinker," which means he/she must observe and reflect on a situation before forming an opinion | I must continue to make learning happen. | • Create opportunities for him/her to participate safely—as in pairs or small groups.
• Pace some activities so there is reflection time included (during break, lunch, or overnight) before participants discuss and share opinions.
• If you can tell by his/her body language that he/she is engaged, listening, reacting, and thinking, consider simply leaving him/her alone. |

Learner's disruptive behavior	Facilitator's personal agenda is triggered	Facilitator recognizes his/her personal agenda and potential behaviors and chooses not to act	Facilitator identifies learner's probable personal agenda	Facilitator mentally reiterates professional agenda	Facilitator chooses to act on professional agenda rather than personal agenda. He or she chooses behaviors that meet the learner's agenda and, by doing so, extinguishes disruptive behavior, and continues the learning.
Withdraws from group interpersonally and/or physically	I must make this person re-engage with the group no matter what.	Directing questions toward him/her to force re-engagement. Make other participants your agents and have them attempt to re-engage him/her.	Is not feeling well Is upset or angry at something that has happened Feels excluded or not listened to	I must continue to make learning happen.	• Ask the person at the next break what is going on and how you can help. Deal with the issue accordingly after that. • Have small groups rotate persons presenting. • Encourage groups to have all members of groups actively involved.
Goes off on tangent; misses the point	How obtuse can someone be?	Make a joke or in some other way belittling him/her for being wrong.	Has misunderstood a point Is on the wrong track Is purposefully being "wrong" to see what I will do	I must continue to make learning happen.	• If possible, find one thing to agree with in what he/she has said. • Affirm and compliment his/her effort to stay engaged with the content. • Say, "That would be a logical assumption; however, the truth is..." • If his/her effort is contrived to see what you will do, the most effective behavior is to address the content of the question rather than take the bait.

Reprinted with permission from Deb Tobey LLC, 2003.

Think About This

Sometimes facilitators can get so focused on extinguishing disruptive behavior that they forget to reinforce that participant's good behavior. Don't forget to react positively when the disruptive participant's behavior lessens (smile or make eye contact, for example). Or, if a talkative participant has remained quiet for a while, ask him or her a question or solicit his or her opinion. It goes back to an old saying: "You can attract more flies with honey than with vinegar!"

Anticipate and Prepare

One last thought on this subject: Be prepared! There are several things you can do prior to facilitating a learning event that can help you anticipate and prepare for the most likely disruptive behaviors.

One thing you can do is review evaluations from previous courses with the same participants, on the same subject, or both. Make note of comments regarding the difficulty of the subject matter and the participants' satisfaction with the facilitation. If possible, get information about the participants from a facilitator who has worked with them in the past. You can also find out from managers—or the participants themselves—about the participants' learning styles, work environments, and enthusiasm about the learning event. Keep up with organizational issues that could be on the participants' minds: downsizing, annual performance appraisals, organizational change efforts, and so forth.

The following suggestions will help you personally be better prepared to manage learner disruptive behavior:

▶ Make a card, poster, or even a Post-it note that says, "My professional agenda is to make learning happen" and put it in a place where you will see it often both at work and even in the classroom.

▶ Make a list of disruptive learner behaviors that are hot buttons for you and make it harder for you to control your reaction. Simply identifying these behaviors and posting the list in your office will help you remember to behave differently.

▶ Make a list of the reactive behaviors that you tend to use most often when a participant behaves in a disruptive manner. Ask a trusted colleague to observe you (in the classroom, in a meeting, in a presentation) and identify the reactive behaviors that he or she sees. Are the two lists the same? Do you exhibit some behaviors that you aren't aware of?

▶ Plan steps you can take to help you recognize that a personal reaction and agenda are about to emerge in a situation and to help you remember to act on your professional agenda (take a deep breath, count to 10, call a break, take a drink of water, and so forth).

Getting It Done

Managing learner disruptive behavior is not easy. It's a challenge that is unique to each facilitator. The key is to recognize the thought process that is occurring and then choose the facilitator behaviors that apply.

The table earlier in this chapter illustrates both the disruptive behavior thought process and potential facilitator actions. Now is the time for you to apply this information to your own facilitation. Part of the table is reproduced in exercise 7-1 to aid in your application activity.

Exercise 7-1. Preparing to deal with disruptive behavior.

Instructions:
1. In the left column, identify learner disruptive behaviors that you will likely encounter during your course.
2. Put an *X* in the space next to the action(s) you plan to use to deal with the disruptive behavior.
3. Add any additional actions you could use in the blank space provided.

Learner's Disruptive Behavior	Facilitator Actions That Meet the Learner's Agenda and Continue the Learning
Side conversation	_____ Behave as if you know the side conversation is class related and ask the participants to add their thoughts.
	_____ If you are lecturing or leading a discussion, slowly move into the part of the room where the disrupters are, continue the lecture or discussion, and don't look at them as you continue.
	_____ Change the pace of the activity; do something active (have participants make flipcharts, put them in small group discussions, etc.).
	_____ Re-form groups.
	_____ At the start of the next session, revisit the class norms/ground rules.
	_____ Other

(continued on page 126)

Exercise 7-1. Preparing to deal with disruptive behavior (continued).

Learner's Disruptive Behavior	Facilitator Actions That Meet the Learner's Agenda and Continue the Learning
Talks too much; monopolizes discussion	_____ If he/she is on the subject, begin talking with him/her and summarize his/her point. Then turn to others and invite their participation: "What does everyone else think?" _____ Avoid eye contact with him/her for a while. _____ If he/she is off target, say, "Great point, but it is beyond the scope of our class . . . Let's talk about this together offline." _____ Put his/her issue on a "parking lot" flipchart. _____ Change the pace of the activity and have participants do solo work for a short time. _____ Other
Complains; is negative about class or organization	_____ Ask if others feel the same way. If they don't, then offer to assist and/or listen to him/her during break. _____ If others do feel the same way, facilitate a "productive tangent." _____ Acknowledge the complaint, then turn group discussion to strategizing how to overcome it. _____ Put the issue on the parking lot. _____ If valid, incorporate it into the action planning to have the learner address the issue. _____ Other
Daydreams; not really "in the class"	_____ Change the current activity to make it more active/involving. _____ If the daydreaming is organization-related and more than one person is doing it, acknowledge it and allow a short discussion, then move on. _____ Talk to him/her privately during a break and ask how the class could be better meeting his/her needs. _____ Frequently link content to the job. _____ Other

Learner's Disruptive Behavior	Facilitator Actions That Meet the Learner's Agenda and Continue the Learning
Heckles the facilitator	_____ Give him/her attention in a learning-oriented way rather than encouraging the heckling. _____ Change the activity so that the participants are interacting with each other rather than with you. _____ If the heckling continues, talk with the person privately. Ask if the class is meeting his/her needs. If not, or if he/she doesn't want to be there, acknowledge and support that within the constraints of the program. If the disruptions continue, send him/her back to the job. _____ Other
Challenges the facilitator on content or technique; "know-it-all"	_____ Give the person the spotlight for a few minutes. _____ Turn the exchange into a discussion by implying that there are multiple points of view and all should be addressed. Ask for other opinions from the rest of the group. _____ Other
Tells jokes or clowns around at inappropriate times	_____ Give him/her attention by reengaging him/her with the content without acknowledging the joking behavior. _____ If the jokes are intended to relieve tension, help the group by bringing up the discomfort directly, or put them in small groups so they can discuss more comfortably. _____ When a joke is funny and at the right time, laugh! _____ Other
Makes an inappropriate remark (sexist, racist, etc.)	_____ Deal with it in front of the group; it cannot be ignored. _____ First, give him/her a chance to retract: "I'm sure you didn't mean that the way it sounded . . ." If he/she does retract, move on. _____ If the person does not retract, say in front of the group "Unfortunately, that view is not in keeping with the values of our organization, and we can't have any more of that." Speak with the person during break—and even report the behavior to his/her manager if necessary. _____ Revisit norms/ground rules for respect of others. _____ Other

(continued on page 128)

Exercise 7-1. Preparing to deal with disruptive behavior (continued).

Learner's Disruptive Behavior	Facilitator Actions That Meet the Learner's Agenda and Continue the Learning
Does other work or reads the newspaper or takes cell phone calls	_____ Speak to him/her during a break and point out that his/her behavior leads you to believe the class is not meeting his/her needs. Ask how the class can better serve his/her needs, and try to do that. _____ Acknowledge the pressure. Negotiate with the participant to appear engaged so that his/her behavior doesn't affect the rest of the group. _____ Offer to have him/her attend another session. _____ Other
Silent, doesn't participate verbally	_____ Create opportunities for him/her to participate safely in pairs or small groups. _____ Pace some activities so there is reflection time included before participants discuss and share opinions. _____ If you can tell by his/her body language that he/she is engaged, listening, reacting, and thinking, consider simply leaving him/her alone. _____ Other
Withdraws from group interpersonally and/or physically	_____ Ask the person at the next break what is going on and how you can help. Deal with the issue accordingly after that. _____ Have small groups rotate persons presenting. _____ Encourage groups to have all members of groups actively involved. _____ Other
Goes off on tangent; misses the point	_____ Find one thing to agree with in what he/she has said. _____ Affirm and compliment his/her effort to stay engaged with the content. _____ Say, "That would be a logical assumption; however, the truth is..." _____ If his/her effort is contrived to see what you will do, the most effective behavior is to address the content of the question rather than take the bait. _____ Other

Reprinted with permission from Deb Tobey LLC, 2003.

You're moving right along on your facilitation journey! The next chapter features how you can use media to enhance and increase learning.

8

Using Media
to Support Learning

■ ■

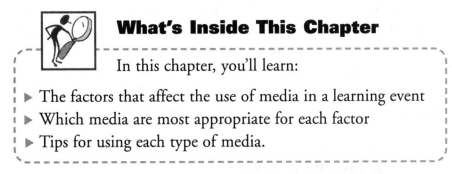

What's Inside This Chapter

In this chapter, you'll learn:

▶ The factors that affect the use of media in a learning event
▶ Which media are most appropriate for each factor
▶ Tips for using each type of media.

Have you ever seen one of those Superbowl Sunday television commercials that was memorable and that you really liked—because it was exceptionally funny or touching—but later couldn't even remember what product was being advertised? That's the potential pitfall in using media in the learning environment as well. What you want the learners to remember and use is the content of your course, not the flashiness of your media. Your course is never about the media you use, no matter how colorful, arresting, or technologically advanced. It's about the learning. The media that you use support and augment the learning.

Media can be effective tools for you as you create a course and strive to make the learning interesting and memorable. In this chapter, the factors that affect the use of media in a learning event are discussed, and the most appropriately used media for each factor are identified. Tips are also provided to assist you in using each type of media.

Basic Rule 35

Learning is about the content, activities, and eventual job performance—not about the media.

For more information on using media, another book in this series, *Presentation Basics* (Rosania, 2003), would also be useful. The discussions in that book are helpful in supporting your use of media, particularly when you are facilitating a content/knowledge/comprehension learning activity or simply making a presentation.

Factors That Affect the Use of Media in Supporting Learning

Selecting media to use as you facilitate a course is one of the most important decisions you'll have to make as you plan a learning event. As you make this decision, remember that the most important rule is to ensure that the media you select will support the learning objectives. Otherwise, the media might distract the learners, actually posing a barrier to learning.

As you're deciding upon which media to use, think about how you like to move throughout the room as you facilitate, how formal your learning event will be, and the level of learner interactivity that you wish to encourage.

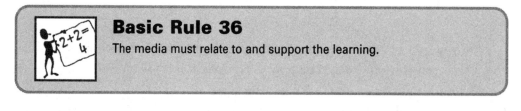

Basic Rule 36

The media must relate to and support the learning.

Facilitator Movement

It was noted in earlier chapters that your ability to move physically around the room and among the learners is important in creating an interactive learning experience. One factor already discussed is the room setup and how it supports—or hinders—your movement. Your media must also support your desired level of movement. If you want to move around quite a bit (which is to be encouraged), you won't want to use media that hampers your movement or keeps you tied to one part of the room or to a piece of equipment.

The media that allow the most movement on the part of the facilitator include written materials; flipcharts; PowerPoint slides, digital presentations, and photographic slides with a remote control; physical props; and videos and DVDs (once you have started them up). The media that allow less movement include whiteboards; overhead transparencies; and PowerPoint, digital presentations, and photographic slides without a remote control.

Basic Rule 37
Media must support the desired amount of facilitator movement.

Level of Formality

The level of formality in your learning event is dictated by a number of factors: the organizational level of your audience, the physical environment, and the organizational culture. The higher the level of the audience (for example, executives as opposed to middle managers and first-line supervisors), the more formal your media should be. The more formal the environment (for example, an executive meeting room with drapes and mahogany furniture as opposed to an employee cafeteria), the more formal your media should be.

And, the more formal the organizational culture, the more formal your media should be. If you're not sure about the formality of the culture, take a look at how everyone dresses (casual, business casual, professional); type of industry (blue collar, white collar); and the type of job your audience works in (office, plant, lab, and so forth).

The more advanced your media technology, the more formal it is. Based on this rule, the order of formality (from most formal to least formal) is:

1. PowerPoint, digital presentations, and photographic slides
2. videos and DVDs
3. overhead transparencies
4. written materials
5. whiteboards
6. flipcharts and easels
7. physical props.

Learner Interactivity With the Media

In an earlier chapter, the fact was presented that learning activities must correspond to the learners' level of knowledge: the more they know, the more active and self-directed the activity. The same characteristic applies to media, and it is recommended that you use media at the highest level of interactivity that is appropriate for the learning involved.

Learner interactivity means how much intellectual or physical involvement learners have with the media (table 8-1). Do the learners have an effect on the message communicated by the media? Do they get to touch the media or manipulate it in some way? Are learners more passive than active in how they are using or interacting with the media?

Basic Rule 38

Media should encourage as much learner interactivity as is appropriate for the learning activity at hand.

Variability in Content Emphasis

Emphasis on course content can vary according to specific learner audiences or as the subject matter itself continues to evolve. Media must allow real-time change and low-cost, low-effort revision when the emphasis on course content varies (table 8-2).

Table 8-1. Interactivity levels associated with different media.

Media With Higher Interactivity	Media With Lower Interactivity
• Handouts with blanks to be filled in • Flipcharts that learners create themselves • Whiteboards that learners write on themselves • Overhead transparencies, whiteboards, flipcharts with blanks that the facilitator fills in as discussion continues • Wallboards that learners write on • Physical props that learners handle	• Overhead transparencies (pre-prepared) • Whiteboards (pre-prepared) • Flipcharts (pre-prepared • Wallboards (pre-prepared) • Handouts with all text filled in • Videos, DVDs • PowerPoint slides, digital presentations, photographic slides • Physical props that only the facilitator handles

Think About This

Your choice of media relative to learner interactivity must also depend on the time of day and course sequence. Your media should be at the high end of interactivity if it is right after lunch or close to the end of the day or if the prior learning activities have been passive to this point. Media can be at the lower end of interactivity if the learners have just completed an intense, active activity, and are in need of a rest.

Table 8-2. Ease of revision for certain media.

Media That Allow Real-Time Change	Media That Allow Low-Cost, Low-Effort Revision	Media That Work Best With Content That Does Not Vary or Evolve
• Flipcharts • Whiteboards • PowerPoint slides	• Flipcharts • Whiteboards • PowerPoint slides • Written materials (handouts) other than books • Physical props	• Videos • DVDs • Books • Photographic slides • Digital presentations • Wallboards

Noted

When learners work alone on an activity, some finish before others and may then become bored or disengaged while waiting for the others to finish. Some facilitators hand out photocopied puzzles, games, or brainteasers to keep these learners occupied while they wait, but these handouts can distract the learners from the subject at hand so you have to reengage them, or they may disturb other learners if they start collaborating on the puzzles, or the learners who work more slowly feel penalized because they didn't get to work on the "fun stuff." Consider instead using handouts that contain additional reading about the subject at hand or creating an additional quiet assignment the faster learners can work on until everyone is finished.

Noted

Have you heard the saying "When you get a new hammer, everything looks like a nail"? These days, Microsoft PowerPoint is that hammer. Don't misunderstand: PowerPoint is a wonderful tool for presenting information. Its many features allow you to make content presentation lively and colorful. Having said that, however, PowerPoint is used too often and too much. Some organizational cultures expect PowerPoint to be used as the only media in courses (too often), and you have probably also seen four-hour courses with 300 PowerPoint slides (too much)! You must choose and use media that best support the learning at the moment. Sometimes that choice is PowerPoint, and many times it is not. Let the learning needs drive the media; don't try to fit the learning to the PowerPoint if it's not a good match.

Basic Rule 39

Don't use just one or two types of media. Use a variety of media in one module or setting.

Generating or Revising Material on the Fly

When your learning activity requires that you (or the learners) brainstorm ideas or generate a list of items on the spot, you need to use a medium that allows you (or them) to write items down in real time. The media that provide this opportunity are flipcharts, fill-in overhead transparencies, fill-in handouts, and whiteboards.

And, just because you'll be working on the fly to list brainstorm ideas, doesn't mean you don't have to be prepared. For example, make sure you have the equipment you need, including the correct writing instruments for the medium you are using. Flipcharts require water-based markers so that the writing doesn't bleed through onto the pages behind, or worse, onto another surface, such as a wall. Whiteboards require dry-erase markers. Use water-based transparency markers (thin point) for overhead transparencies. Here's what happens if you use the wrong marker:

▶ Dry-erase markers used on flipcharts results in not enough ink being applied, which causes faded lettering that is hard to see.

▶ Water-based markers used on whiteboards can't be erased on the spot; they require special cleaning.

▶ Regular water-based markers (instead of overhead transparency markers) used on overhead transparencies results in fading and smearing, so the overhead is unreadable.

Need for Continued Visibility

In many learning events, the facilitator wants not only to save media that have been produced during the class, but also to keep it visible as an ongoing record of what the learners have produced. This method helps learners review concepts, look back at prior events, and see progress that has been made. Flipcharts and wallboards posted on the wall work very well for this need. Whiteboards work well if there are several of them in your room.

Portability

Sometimes you must take your learning materials on the road to a different site or sometimes simply to a different room in your facility. In this case, ease of portability becomes a factor. Part of your portability decision rests on what media or technology is already be available at the facility you'll be using.

Overhead transparencies are extremely portable, especially if the facility you will use already has a projector and screen. PowerPoint and digital presentations are very portable on a laptop computer if the room you'll be using is equipped with an LCD projector or computer data projector. Though relatively expensive, there are now small computer projectors that are easy to transport. Videos and DVDs likewise are very portable if there is equipment available at your site. All of these items become much less portable if there is no audiovisual equipment at your site. The best option in this case is to take a portable overhead projector with you or a compact computer projector and laptop.

Flipcharts are not very portable; even the supposedly "easy to carry" charts and easels on the market aren't! (Ask anyone who has had to lug flipcharts around.) The best option is to request a flipchart and easel at the site or to use blank overhead transparencies in place of a flipchart. If you have many handouts, these are not very portable either and can be quite heavy. The best bet in this case is to use a rolling suitcase to carry them—even for a short trip from the trunk of your car into the building!

Alternatively, you can ship materials and equipment ahead of time. If you ship materials, get the name of the person who should be receiving your shipment. Then, follow up to be sure the material arrived and will be at the room.

Think About This

Facilitators who must move to multiple sites should have a backup plan in case the expected media arrangement is unavailable. In other words, know what you will do ahead of time if you must switch to a different way of presenting information. You can even bring an alternative set of media with you; for example, if you plan to use PowerPoint, bring a set of overhead transparencies of the PowerPoint slides, as well as a set of printouts that you can photocopy and distribute if worse comes to worst. Many facilitators have been saved more than once by having such a contingency plan ready to go.

Basic Rule 40
Always have a media backup plan.

Physical Environment

The physical environment of the space you are working in will affect your use of media also. The larger the room, the "larger" your media should be—typically overhead transparencies or PowerPoint slides. If columns or other barriers hamper visibility, multiple flipcharts stationed at multiple points help all learners feel involved. If you want to keep a record of work done, the wall surfaces must be amenable to tape or self-stick flipcharts or pushpins. The lighting options available will dictate whether it is appropriate (and advisable) to use media such as slides, videos, PowerPoint, or overhead transparencies that require dimmed room lighting.

Think About This

Keep the room as brightly lit as you can when you're projecting media. Some rooms allow you to dim only the lights in the vicinity of the projection screen while keeping the rest of the room fairly bright. Under no circumstances turn out the lights right after lunch!

A large room or poor acoustics dictate use of a microphone. If you must use a microphone in a large space, use a lavaliere microphone with a power pack that clips to your clothing. You can then move about the room if necessary, unlike with a stationary microphone at a podium. Another tip is to wear clothing that will make attaching the microphone and power pack easy (for example, a jacket with a lapel for the microphone and a pocket for the power pack).

A Word About Physical Props

To paraphrase, sometimes a prop or object lesson is worth a thousand words. Physical props are especially useful in illustrating analogies. Seeing or handling a prop makes learning much more meaningful to visual and kinesthetic learners. Here are a few quick examples:

▶ Using a Slinky to illustrate cause and effect
▶ Having learners build something with Tinkertoys or LEGO building blocks to demonstrate teamwork or effective planning
▶ Using an actual burlap sack to illustrate the negative effect of "gunny-sacking" complaints in a conflict situation.

The possibilities are limited only by your imagination and creativity. And, remember the discussion in chapter 4 about personalizing the learning to fit your style? If you have a talent or hobby, this is the place to use it to illustrate a learning point. For example, there was a description in chapter 4 about a musician who uses music and instruments to illustrate synergy and teamwork. Amateur magicians can use magic tricks to illustrate learning points, and so on.

Using Copyrighted Material

Think again before you consider making a transparency or handout of a "Dilbert" cartoon, playing a Kenny G compact disc for background music, videotaping a sketch from "Saturday Night Live" to show during a course; or checking out the motion picture "12 Angry Men" from the video/DVD store and showing it to a group. Don't do it without checking with your legal department. Doing these things without permission of the publisher or licenser is a potential violation of copyright law. Getting permission can sometimes be worth the trouble, so when it's important for your learning event, contact the publisher or licenser of the material and ask for permission.

Alternatively, you can make your own cartoons with clipart (available on CDs or on the Internet). Some music stores offer generic, instrumental CDs that do not have copyright implications (and for a learning environment, instrumental music is the only way to go because music with lyrics distracts from the learning environment). And, there are many, many training videos/DVDs that can be rented or purchased specifically for a learning event.

Where to Begin?

You've been introduced to a great deal of material in this chapter. You'll find it all summarized in table 8-3, which can serve as a convenient reference for you as you plan to facilitate various learning events.

Table 8-3. Tips for using media to support learning.

Media Type	When to Use	Tips	Pluses and Minuses
Flipcharts and Easels	• Informal learning events • To generate materials/items on the spot • When you need to keep the lights on	• Make your writing legible and large (six lines per page, letters 2 inches high). • Keep a record of progress throughout the learning event. • Use headings on media to keep your talk organized. • Vary colors: Blue and black lettering are most easily seen; green and red can mean "pro" and "con" or "do" and "don't"; color-blind learners can't differentiate green and red. • Leave blank pages in between so the text of the next page can't be seen. • If right-handed, stand to left of chart; if left-handed, stand to right. • Write notes to yourself in light pencil on the pages. • Make tabs out of Post-it notes or tape, so you can flip easily to the desired page. • "Touch, turn, talk": Write on the chart (and don't talk to the chart while writing), turn, then speak.	+ Informality creates comfortable environment + Good for smallish rooms + Learners can make their own for activities/presentations − Don't work well in large rooms; can't be seen by learners who are more than 30 feet away − Must have legible handwriting − Not good for more formal groups or groups who expect a presentation supported by technology

(continued on page 140)

Table 8-3. Tips for using media to support learning (continued).

Media Type	When to Use	Tips	Pluses and Minuses
Overhead Transparencies	• Informal learning events • Generate material/items on the spot on blank ones • Multiple sites	• Moderate-sized room • If writing on media on the fly, be legible • Multiple colors; same cautions as with flipcharts • Use large fonts and graphics • Clean the glass before using • Focus the projector without revealing your transparencies by placing a coin with ridged edges on the glass • Talk to learners, not to the glass in front of you or screen behind you • Point out items on the transparency on the glass, not on the screen behind you • Turn off projector when finished with the content on that transparency and you want to direct attention elsewhere and when changing transparencies to avoid glare • Revelation technique: Place a piece of paper under the transparency and slide it slowly to reveal one item at a time	+ Learners can make their own for activities or presentations + Useful for learning events you facilitate multiple times + Can carry with you easily to multiple sites − Need fairly low room light − Machine could break down or bulb can fail − "Keystone" effect of projection screen − Can trip over cords − If you have too many transparencies, the setup creates a physical barrier for too long a time because you must stand at the projector
Whiteboards	• Informal learning events • Generate material or brainstorm items on the spot	• Use when you need to keep the lights on. • Keep a record of progress throughout the learning event, if you have enough boards. • Make your writing legible and large (six lines per page, letters 2 inches high). • Use headings on it to keep your talk organized. • Can use it to jot notes during a discussion.	+ Learners can use for activities/presentations + Good for smallish rooms − Can't move the board around the room − Don't work well in large rooms; can't be seen by learners who are more than 30 feet away

Media Type	When to Use	Tips	Pluses and Minuses
Whiteboards (continued)		• Vary colors: blue and black are most easily seen; green and red can mean "pro" and "con" or "do" and "don't"; color-blind learners can't differentiate green and red. • "Touch, turn, talk": Write on the board (and don't talk to the board while writing), turn, then speak. • Use dry-erase markers.	
PowerPoint Slides, Digital Presentations, or Photographic Slides	• Good for formal learning events • Useful for learning events you facilitate multiple times	• Multiple colors; same cautions as with flipcharts • Use large, sans serif fonts • Use graphics • Point out items on the screen, not on the screen behind you • Use the revelation technique: Animate and build the content item by item on the screen • Talk to learners, not the screen behind you • Don't use these media too often or too much	+ Can be eye-catching and very visual + Works in large room with large groups + Easily transportable on a laptop or on floppy disk, CD, or memory chip where a computer and LCD projector are available already + Content is easily modified − Technology can break down − Challenging to add items on the fly during the learning event − Need low room light − Learners may be weary of too many PowerPoint presentations
Videos and DVDs	• Use for behavioral modeling (watch someone doing right/wrong) • Use for situational/case analysis	• Make sure there are enough monitors for all to see. • Stop to discuss after a maximum of 15 minutes; then start up again. • Be sure settings and clothing in film are not too dated; could be distracting.	+ Excellent as a way to provide media variety + Works well for content that doesn't evolve or fluctuate + Works well to examine skills; can show either "do" or "don't" − Passive medium − Can be used for too long ("the electronic babysitter")

(continued on page 142)

Table 8-3. Tips for using media to support learning (continued).

Media Type	When to Use	Tips	Pluses and Minuses
Written Materials	• When you want learners to have references • When learners must work alone	• Use colors and graphics as discussed above. • Provide white space for note taking. • Leave blanks for structured note taking. • Give out as they are needed so learners don't read ahead. • Can make hard copies of PowerPoint and digital presentations for later reference.	+ Gives more detailed information for later reference + Great for visual learners – Doesn't resonate with auditory learners
Props and Objects	• When you want to make a point especially memorable	• Use your imagination. • Be creative. • Use props that are natural and comfortable for you. • Take advantage of your own special talents. • Make sure the illustration or analogy is accurate and easily understood.	+ Memorable + Fun – Not very portable
Wallboards	• When you want learners to be able to refer to a graphically produced visual • As a content organization tool for complex material	• Laminate them so they can be written on • Use color to delineate content relationships • Better in a moderate-sized room • Use as a map to manage content, focus, and transitions • Have them professionally prepared • Learners can post comments and questions by content area	+ Maintains content continuity + Meets needs of visual and kinesthetic learners + Useful for global thinkers – Not effective for auditory learners – Does not work with large groups or rooms – Difficult to modify in real time

Reprinted with permission from Deb Tobey LLC, 2003.

Getting It Done

Table 8-3 provided some additional tips and techniques that will aid you in using media to support learning. Use it as you complete the checklist in exercise 8-1, which allows you to apply the various media implications and decisions to your own situations.

Exercise 8-1. Thinking about how to use media to support learning.

Use the checklist below to make sure you have considered all media implications when you prepare to facilitate a course or module.

The media you've selected:

_____ Incorporates the appropriate amount of movement for the learning activity and my facilitator style

Notes:

_____ Maintains an appropriate level of formality/informality

Notes:

_____ Provides an appropriate level of learner intellectual interactivity

Notes:

_____ Offers an appropriate level of learner physical interactivity

Notes:

_____ Includes an appropriate level of interactivity for the time of day

Notes:

_____ Involves an appropriate amount of light for the room and time of day

Notes:

_____ Is the correct medium for variability and evolution of content emphasis

Notes:

_____ Is appropriately portable

Notes:

(continued on page 144)

Exercise 8-1. Thinking about how to use media to support learning (continued).

You've prepared for facilitating using media by:

_____ Incorporating a variety of media into the course

Notes:

_____ Having the right markers for the media

Notes:

_____ Assessing the physical environment and matching the best media to the environment

Notes:

_____ Planning for backup media, just in case

Notes:

_____ Obtaining permission for use of material obtained

Notes:

In this chapter, you were introduced to the many variables and components inherent in using media for effective learning facilitation. Chapter 9 will assist you in assessing your skill levels and in the skill levels of other facilitators that you supervise or hire.

9

Assessing Facilitation
Quality

■ ■

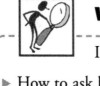

What's Inside This Chapter

In this chapter, you'll learn:

▶ How to ask learners for feedback on facilitation quality
▶ The observation methods used to obtain feedback
▶ How to analyze performance on activities, tests, and assessments to obtain feedback
▶ About level 1 and 2 evaluations for facilitator feedback.

All facilitators want to know how they are doing. You are in the late afternoon of the first day of a two-day program. It is natural—and professional—to want to know how things are going. After all, it is your responsibility to make learning happen. So, is it happening? How can you find out?

Kirkpatrick (1994) indicates that there are four levels of evaluation. These are reaction (level 1), learning (level 2), behavior (level 3), and results (level 4). For facilitators, levels 1 and 2 provide feedback within the learning experience. Level 1 is a measure of learner satisfaction; that is, how participants react to their experience. Level 2 addresses whether learning took place. Was there a knowledge shift? As a

Noted

Effective facilitators are less concerned about whether the learners are having a good time than about whether learning is happening. Fun does not equate learning or application to the job. Feedback should be sought to ensure that learning is always foremost, but the facilitator must keep in mind the limitations and strengths of the various ways of eliciting feedback from the learners.

result of the learning, did skills increase? Can the learner demonstrate the new behaviors in the learning experience? To provide this feedback, instruments are developed to solicit feedback and to assess if learning took place. These instruments are part of the design/development process. These aspects of evaluation as they relate to the facilitator are discussed later in this chapter.

Asking for Feedback

Yes, a facilitator can ask the group or individual learners for feedback, either verbal or written. When you ask learners for feedback, you are making some assumptions:

- ▶ They are willing to give feedback.
- ▶ They know enough about facilitation to provide meaningful feedback.
- ▶ You know how to ask or frame the questions that will provide meaningful feedback.
- ▶ You are willing to make changes based on the feedback.
- ▶ The feedback received is representative of a larger group of learners participating in this delivery.

Basic Rule 41
If you are not going to act on the feedback, do not solicit it.

When giving verbal feedback, learners often have a difficult time providing honest, constructive feedback. There is group pressure not to be too critical. When asked, they may respond, "Things are going fine," or "Everything is going great." In some cases, they point out things beyond your control, such as "PowerPoint slides need to be more creative," or "Use a different color or larger text on the slides," or "Guides have misspelled words," or "Content is not relevant to my job." These issues are important because they are interfering with learning, but this feedback doesn't help you be a better facilitator at that precise moment. When this happens, take this feedback to the course designer/developer so he or she can make appropriate changes. You want to facilitate this change so you have a quality learning experience to facilitate.

One organization asks for verbal feedback for the end-of-course evaluation. Learners are asked to rate the course from 1–10 (with 10 being the highest), and they are asked for specific comments. The facilitator always starts with a learner who seems to be having a good experience. This learner's answer usually nets a high rating and positive comments. As subsequent learners respond individually, the peer pressure to maintain the comments and rating is significant. So, does this evaluation provide good and reliable information? No! Does it result in good ratings for the facilitators and program? Yes! Does it produce valuable feedback? No!

Verbal feedback is further complicated by your role of facilitator, which is one of perceived influence and power. This misperception limits your ability to get honest feedback. In short, learners don't want to say anything that may result in a bad perception of them. (By the way, the amount of influence and power learners think facilitators have with the learners' managers is surprising. Would that it were so!)

Basic Rule 42
In general, verbal feedback does not provide reliable or useful information.

By using a form of written, anonymous feedback, you improve your chances of getting reliable information, but not by much. If questions are open-ended, you must frame them so there is little room for interpretation. Such questions are difficult to write. Once the feedback is received, you must then read each survey and do some kind of thematic analysis to see where things are going well and where changes are required. If you develop a scaled response instrument (statements with a rating scale, say from 1–4 with a descriptor for each rating number), you must contend

Noted

In many cases, the course designer/developer has provided you with an interim evaluation instrument you can use to gather feedback.

with rater bias (learners' tendency to rate high) and still identify the areas that are going well and not so well. And, unless you add places for comments, this approach provides only a relative score. You must interpret the score and determine actions to take.

Observation

Peer observation is a good method for you to get feedback on your facilitation skills. You can use the facilitation/presentation assessment instrument previously introduced in exercise 3-2 and ask a trusted peer to observe a part of the course you're facilitating. If you use this approach, remember these things:

▶ The peer evaluator must be a high-performing facilitator.
▶ The peer evaluator must be familiar with the evaluation instrument.
▶ The peer evaluator must have your developmental interests in mind.
▶ You must have confidence in your peer's evaluation of you.
▶ You must not facilitate differently when the peer evaluator is observing your facilitation.
▶ You must be willing to use the feedback.

Think About This

Some training rooms have an observation booth where others can unobtrusively view the facilitator and learners. This feature provides an excellent opportunity to reduce the bias that would be introduced if you tend to perform differently when you know you're being observed.

Another option is to videotape your facilitation. You can tape the entire learning event or particular modules you are concerned about. You then have the option of reviewing the video by yourself or with a trusted peer. You could combine this activity with the use of an objective instrument (such as the facilitation/presentation assessment in exercise 3-2) to help carry out a complete review with less subjectivity.

Level 1 Evaluation

End-of-course evaluations are seen by some as "smile sheets" that provide little value. Others see them as an opportunity to gain insights into program and facilitator strengths and development/revision areas. The factors making the level 1 evaluation more usable include the following:

▶ Is it customized to the course and particular delivery?

▶ Are the learning objectives included?

▶ Is there sufficient detail to make a decision regarding program content, facilitator skills, logistics, and so forth?

▶ Is the information used for feedback to the facilitator, program administrator, or logistical coordinator?

▶ Is there a separate section relating to the facilitator's skills?

▶ Are all areas of the instrument relevant?

All of these issues affect the relevance and use of the level 1 evaluation instrument. There are definitely level 1 areas that can provide feedback to the facilitator.

First, the questions concerning course learning objectives tell you the extent to which the learners say the course objectives were met. This assumes the instrument is of the scaled response type. If a large proportion of the learners respond that certain objectives were not met, this indicates a lapse in content or facilitation of the content.

Some research can tell you which of these factors need to be addressed. Many times as facilitators get behind schedule, they make up time by skimming through content. In other cases, the content was more difficult for the facilitator and therefore not as well "presented" to the learners.

Basic Rule 43

Learner feedback on how well course objectives were met provides insights into the quality of facilitation.

The other critical area on the level 1 evaluation for you as a facilitator is the section dealing directly with your capabilities. Here's a list of several areas related to facilitators that you will find on many level 1 instruments:

▶ promoted an environment of learning

▶ presented clearly to assist the participants' understanding

- demonstrated knowledge of the subject matter
- provided feedback effectively to participants
- responded well to questions
- presented content in an appropriate sequence
- promoted participant discussion and involvement
- kept the discussion on topic and activities on track
- coached participants on learning activities.

As you can see, specific feedback in this level of detail can provide specific areas for facilitator development or areas of strength to be maintained. The intent of feedback is to identify areas to hone your skills. This includes not only areas for development, but also areas in which you perform well so you can continue to strengthen those skills.

Think About This

The use of level 1 evaluation is delivery specific. Content, design, or facilitation changes should not be made based on the feedback for only one or two deliveries. Instead, collect level 1 evaluation data for several courses you facilitate and look for trends. Gathering more information increases reliability for decision making.

Level 2 Evaluation

Level 2 evaluation depends on activities, tests, and assessments to evaluate whether participants have learned (shift in knowledge) and whether they can demonstrate the skill or behavior within the learning experience. Level 2 is relevant to you because as a facilitator you are responsible for making sure learning happens.

Performance on Activities

Learners' performance on learning activities can provide you with feedback as to how well you are explaining content of the course or instructions.

If learners are struggling with providing accurate and complete responses to the activities, it may be a sign that the content was not covered adequately. If there is a

Noted

Other areas that are addressed in many level 1 evaluations include course content (of which objectives are a part), course methodology, environment, and course administration. Many level 1 instruments also have a place for general comments and an item asking if the learner would recommend the course to a peer.

content issue, you may need to revisit that part of the material to ensure adequate learning takes place.

If they are asking questions regarding the meaning or application of the content, there is the real possibility that they lack the knowledge or skill to complete the activity. Likewise, if several learners are asking questions about what is expected of them, the instructions were probably not adequately explained or posted. All these responses are feedback on your facilitation.

Performance on Tests

The learners' performance on knowledge tests is a clear indication of the extent that the learners are grasping the material. By doing a quick item analysis, you can isolate the content area where learners have the most difficulty. Could it be a test question format? Yes, it could. Could it be that the course content was not included in the leader's guide? Yes, it could. Could it be that the facilitator did not adequately cover, explain, or teach the content? Yes, it could. In any case, the learners have not acquired the content. Your job is to determine the source of the problem and correct it.

Performance on Assessments

Observation with supporting checklists can also be used to evaluate learners' performance on case studies, role plays, and other assessments that serve as objective instruments that you or a peer evaluator are using to evaluate learners' performance. Again, where are the areas of difficulty and what is the causal factor? Then, address the cause.

Noted

Item analysis is a method by which you examine each item on the test/instrument and count the number of correct and incorrect answers to that item. For example, for a multiple choice test where there are 20 learners and the answer to question 5 is A, you count the number who responded A and the number responding B, C, or D. Several learners missing the same question or providing the same wrong answer indicates the content area for you to examine regarding the need for more emphasis or concentration.

Getting It Done

Developing ways to collect and identify feedback is a skill unto itself. Use exercise 9-1 to identify some items on an evaluation instrument that you might use to collect feedback on your facilitation skills.

Below is a sample level 1 evaluation instrument. Highlight the sections you think are important and would like to use for your level 1 evaluation.

COURSE INFORMATION

Course Title: _____   Facilitator: _____

Job Classification (check one):

___Administrative/Hourly   ___Professional   ___Supervisor   ___Manager

___Other (write in): _____

The statements below concern specific aspects of this course. Please indicate to what extent you agree with each statement by circling the appropriate number. Please use the following scale:

Strongly Disagree = 1   Disagree = 2   Agree = 3   Strongly Agree = 4

I. Course Content				
Objectives were clearly explained.	1	2	3	4
Objectives stated were met; the participant will be able to:				
• Objective 1:	1	2	3	4
• Objective 2:	1	2	3	4
• Objective 3:	1	2	3	4
• Objective 4:	1	2	3	4
Material was well organized.	1	2	3	4
Content is relevant to my job.	1	2	3	4

II. Course Methodology
The following activities/materials helped me to understand the content and to achieve the objectives:

Participant's workbook	1	2	3	4
Class discussions	1	2	3	4
Individual exercises and/or activities	1	2	3	4
Small group/team discussions and activities	1	2	3	4
Media (flipcharts, PowerPoint slides, videos, tapes, etc.)	1	2	3	4

(continued on page 154)

Exercise 9-1. Selecting elements for a level 1 evaluation instrument (continued).

III. Instructor/Facilitator

Promoted an environment of learning	1	2	3	4
Presented clearly to assist my understanding	1	2	3	4
Demonstrated knowledge of the subject matter	1	2	3	4
Provided feedback effectively to participants	1	2	3	4
Responded well to questions	1	2	3	4
Presented content in an appropriate sequence	1	2	3	4
Promoted participant discussion and involvement	1	2	3	4
Kept the discussion on topic and activities on track	1	2	3	4

IV. Environment/Course Administration

The class was free of external distractions.	1	2	3	4
The room was neat and clean.	1	2	3	4
The promotional material accurately represents course content.	1	2	3	4
The registration process is effective.	1	2	3	4

V. General

Course pace was (✓)

_____ Too slow   _____ About right   _____ Too fast

Please indicate (✓) the rating that best reflects your overall evaluation of this session.

_____ Poor   _____ Fair   _____ Good   _____ Excellent

Would your recommend this course to your peers (✓)? _____ Yes _____ No

Why, or why not?_____

_____

Your suggestions for improvement: _____

_____

Other comments:_____

_____

Thank you for taking the time to share your comments and reactions to your learning experience.

Reprinted with permission from Performance Advantage Group, 1999.

Now, turn to exercise 9-2 to create your own evaluation instrument and enhance your ability to design ways to collect and use feedback on your facilitation skills.

Exercise 9-2. Developing an evaluation instrument.

In the space below, try your hand at developing a written instrument to solicit feedback from learners. Assume that you are about halfway through a three-day program. Be sure to cover such topics as pace, sequence of the content, skill/knowledge acquisition and application, value of activities, various aspects of your skills as a facilitator, and so forth.

Facilitators of learning experiences do not exist in an organizational vacuum. What you do and how you do it contribute to performance, which ultimately contributes to your organization's bottom line. In the final chapter, you'll explore some points about the facilitator's critical role in the organization. This chapter also offers additional advice on facilitator effectiveness.

10

A Final Note

■ ■

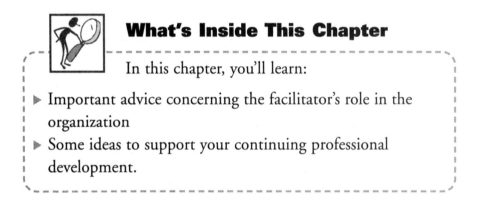

What's Inside This Chapter

In this chapter, you'll learn:

▶ Important advice concerning the facilitator's role in the organization
▶ Some ideas to support your continuing professional development.

Continuous learning is critical to success on the individual, business unit, and organizational levels. An organization's only sustainable advantage is its human capital. How that human capital is continually developed to address corporate and individual needs is a critical factor leading to ultimate success or failure. This is a huge issue for organizations in general and HRD in particular.

This issue encompasses many issues that are beyond the scope of this book, but you, the facilitator of learning, can play a key role. Your role goes beyond just presenting information in a two-day event. Your role is to make learning happen and to assist in having that learning applied on the job. Your role should not and cannot stop at the classroom door. As a facilitator, you influence the learners and prepare the environment to support the new knowledge, skills, and behaviors on the job. It is a large responsibility with critical results.

To fulfill your role with excellence, you must continue to develop your competencies as a professional. Like any field, the HRD profession is continuing to change. There are new approaches to learning, new techniques, new facilitation skills, and ever-changing delivery methods.

In addition, you must continue to develop your knowledge of the organization and industry of which you are a part. This is a dynamic environment with changing products, strategies, competitors, legal/regulatory requirements, and customer requirements, to mention just a few. To not only facilitate content, but also to support transfer, you need to continue to stay abreast of these changes. In addition, you need to continue to develop your general business sense to maintain your credibility in your organization and stay abreast of new business jargon and concepts. It is amazing how many doors will open for you.

The best facilitators are also subject matter experts. The days of a facilitator simply memorizing and delivering a script are past. You must be able to speak from your knowledge and experience. You must be able to respond to content questions beyond the superficial. And, you must be able to help the learners apply the content to their job situation.

That's not to say that you do not need to know the material in the leader's guide. You do, but that's only the beginning. You need to be able to go beyond the guide. Your credibility and that of your department are at stake. You must be able to take the content deeper, to extend the activities beyond where the learners are, and to coach for transfer.

Basically, your job as facilitator is to

▶ support and increase performance of the individual, business unit, and organization
▶ help individuals and the organization solve business problems and meet objectives
▶ go beyond the classroom to support transfer of learning to the workplace
▶ make learning happen.

Your job is *not*

▶ to limit learning to the classroom
▶ to be popular or liked, nor is it to meet your personal needs of being in the limelight, being right, or acting the part of expert.

To support you in your continuous learning, consult the Additional Resources section of this book for additional reference material. The references are organized into categories to help you find the sources you need. This list is not exhaustive, but it will build on what you've learned in this book, starting you on the road to excellence in facilitation.

Getting It Done

You can excel in your work by honing your skills and by strengthening a major weakness. Top performers continually develop themselves whether by readings, seminars, workshops, job assignments, coaching, and so forth.

Exercise 10-1 is a development plan so you can continue your progress for excellence in performance.

Exercise 10-1. Continue your professional development.

In the spaces provided below:

1. Describe one strength you want to hone and one weakness you want to overcome.
2. Identify the method for development and required resources.
3. Establish a timeline for your development activities.
4. Determine the required feedback so you will know the extent of your improvement.

Describe one strength:

_____

_____

_____

_____

Method for Development	Resources	Timeline	Feedback

(continued on page 160)

Exercise 10-1. Continue your professional development (continued).

Describe one weakness:

_____

_____

_____

_____

Method for Development	Resources	Timeline	Feedback

Best wishes on your future facilitations!

References

Carliner, S. (2003). *Training Design Basics.* Alexandria, VA: ASTD.

Kirkpatrick, D. (1994). *Evaluating Training Programs: The Four Levels.* San Francisco: Berrett-Koehler.

Knowles, M. (1988). *The Modern Practice of Adult Education: From Pedagogy to Androgogy.* Englewood Cliffs, NJ: Cambridge Book Company.

———. (1990). *The Adult Learner: A Neglected Species,* 4th edition. Houston: Gulf Publishing.

Mitchell, G. (1998). *The Trainer's Handbook: The AMA Guide to Effective Training,* 3d edition. New York: AMACOM.

Nadler, L., and Z. Nadler. (1994). *Designing Training Programs: The Critical Events Mode,* 2d edition. Houston: Gulf Publishing.

Rosania, R. (2003). *Presentation Basics.* Alexandria, VA: ASTD.

Rose, C. (1987). *Accelerated Learning.* New York: Bantam Dell.

Additional Resources

■ ■

Adult Learning

Knowles, M., E.F. Holton, and R.A. Swanson. (1998). *The Adult Learner: The Definitive Classic in Adult Education and Human Resource Development,* 5th edition. Houston: Gulf Publishing.

Merriam, S.B., editor. (2001). *New Directions for Adult and Continuing Education.* San Francisco: Jossey-Bass.

Merriam, S.B., and R.S. Cafarella. (1998). *Learning in Adulthood: A Comprehensive Guide.* San Francisco: Jossey-Bass.

Vella, J. (2002). *Learning to Listen, Learning to Teach: The Power of Dialogue in Educating Adults.* San Francisco: Jossey-Bass.

Facilitator Competencies and Facilitation Skills

Bentley, T. (1994). *Facilitation: Providing Opportunities for Learning.* New York: McGraw-Hill.

Eitington, J.E. (2001). *The Winning Trainer: Winning Ways to Involve People in Learning,* 4th edition. Burlington, MA: Butterworth-Heinemann.

Hunter, D., A. Bailey, and B. Taylor. (1995). *The Art of Facilitation.* Tucson, AZ: Fisher Books.

Justice, T., and D.W. Jamieson. (1999). *The Facilitator's Fieldbook.* New York: AMACOM.

Kearney, L. (1995). *The Facilitator's Toolkit.* Amherst, MA: HRD Press.

Kinlaw, D. (1996). *Facilitation Skills: The ASTD Trainer's Sourcebook.* New York: McGraw-Hill Trade.

Leatherman, D. (1990). *The Training Trilogy: Facilitation Skills.* Amherst, MA: HRD Press.

Rumsey, T.A. (1996). *Not Just Games: Strategic Uses of Experiential Learning to Drive Business Results.* Dubuque, IA: Kendall-Hunt.

Shapiro, L.T. (1995). *Training Effectiveness Handbook.* New York: McGraw-Hill.

Wheeling, S.A. (1990). *Facilitating Training Groups.* New York: Praeger.

Instructional Design and Learning Activity Development

Anglin, G. (1991). *Instructional Technology: Past, Present, and Future.* Englewood, CO: Libraries Unlimited.

Barca, M., and K. Cobb. (1994). *Beginnings & Endings: Creative Warm-Ups & Closure Activities.* Amherst, MA: HRD Press.

Broad, M., and J. Newstron. (1992). *Transfer of Training.* Reading, MA: Addison-Wesley.

Charney, C., and K. Conway. (1998). *The Trainer's Tool Kit.* New York: AMA-COM.

Clark, R. (1989). *Developing Technical Training: A Structured Approach for the Development of Classroom and Computer-Based Instructional Materials.* Reading, MA: Addison-Wesley.

Jones, K. (1997). *Creative Events for Trainers.* New York: McGraw-Hill.

Kolb, D., and D. Smith. (1986). *Learning Style Inventory: User's Guide.* Boston: McBer & Company.

Leatherman, D. (1990). *The Training Trilogy: Designing Programs.* Amherst, MA: HRD Press.

Newstron, J.W., and E.E. Scannell. (1980). *Games Trainers Play.* New York: McGraw-Hill.

———. (1991). *Still More Games Trainers Play.* New York: McGraw-Hill.

———. (1993). *More Games Trainers Play.* New York: McGraw-Hill.

———. (1994). *Even More Games Trainers Play.* New York: McGraw-Hill.

Pfeiffer, J.W., and J.E. Jones. (1976–present). *The Annual Handbook for Group Facilitators.* San Francisco: Jossey Bass.

Phillips, J., and M.L. Broad. (1997). *In Action: Transferring Learning to the Workplace.* Alexandria, VA: ASTD.

Silberman, M. (1990). *Active Training: Handbook of Techniques, Designs, Case Examples, and Tips.* New York: Lexington Books.

Silberman, M., and K. Lawson. (1995). *101 Ways to Make Training Active.* San Diego: Pfeiffer.

Measurement and Evaluation

Brinkerhoff, R.O. (1987). *Achieving Results from Training.* San Francisco: Jossey-Bass.

Dixon, N. (1990). *Evaluation: A Tool for Improving Quality.* San Diego: University Associates.

Kirkpatrick, D.L. (1994). *Evaluating Training Programs: The Four Levels.* San Francisco: Berrett-Koehler Publishers.

Phillips, J. (1994). *In Action: Measuring Return-on-Investment.* Alexandria, VA: ASTD.

———. (1996). *Accountability in Human Resource Management.* Houston: Gulf Publishing.

———. (1997). *Handbook of Training Evaluation and Measurement Methods,* 3d edition. Houston: Gulf Publishing.

Robinson, D.G., and J.C. Robinson. (1989). *Training for Impact: How to Link Training to Business Needs and Measure the Results.* San Francisco: Jossey-Bass.

Swanson, R., and E. Holton. (1999). *Results? How to Assess Performance, Learning, and Perceptions in Organizations.* San Francisco: Berrett-Koehler Publishers.

Needs Analysis

Leatherman, D. (1990). *The Training Trilogy: Assessing Needs.* Amherst, MA: HRD Press.

Mager, R.F., and P. Pipe. (1989). *Analyzing Performance Problems.* Belmont, CA: Pittman Learning.

Phillips, J., and E.F. Holton III. (1995). *In Action: Conducting Needs Assessment.* Alexandria, VA: ASTD.

Rossett, A. (1987). *Training Needs Assessment.* New York: Educational Technology Publishers.

Swanson, R. (1996). *Analysis for Improving Performance.* San Francisco: Berrett-Koehler Publishers.

Zemke, R., and T. Kramlinger. (1982). *Figuring Things Out: A Trainer's Guide to Needs & Task Analysis.* Reading, MA: Addison-Wesley.

Presentation Skills

Becker, D., and P.B. Becker. (1994). *Powerful Presentation Skills.* Chicago: Irwin Professional Publishing.

Burn, B.E. (1996). *Flip Chart Power: Secrets of the Masters.* San Francisco: Jossey-Bass/Pfeiffer.

Jolles, R.L. (2000). *How to Run Seminars and Workshops: Presentation Skills for Consultants, Trainers, and Teachers.* New York: John Wiley & Sons.

Peoples, D.A. (1997). *Presentations Plus: David Peoples' Proven Techniques,* revised edition. New York: John Wiley & Sons.

Pike, R., and D. Arch. (1997). *Dealing With Difficult Participants: 127 Practical Strategies for Minimizing Resistance and Maximizing Results in Your Presentations.* San Francisco: Jossey-Bass.

Silberman, M., and K. Clark. (1999). *101 Ways to Make Meetings Active: Surefire Ideas to Engage Your Group.* San Francisco: Jossey-Bass/Pfeiffer.

Stettner, M. (2002). *Mastering Business Presentations.* McLean, VA: National Institute of Business Management.

Zelazny, G. (1999). *Say It With Presentations: How to Design and Deliver Successful Business Presentations.* New York: McGraw-Hill Trade.

Strategic HRD

Craig, R. (1987). *Training and Development Handbook,* 3d edition. New York: McGraw-Hill.

Gilley, J., and A. Maycunich. (1998). *Strategically Integrated HRD: Partnering to Maximize Organizational Performance.* Reading, MA: Addison-Wesley.

Hudson, W. (1993). *Intellectual Capital: How to Build It, Enhance It, Use It.* New York: John Wiley & Sons.

Svenson, R.A., M.J. Rinderer, and R. Svenson. (1992). *The Training and Development Strategic Plan Workbook.* Englewood Cliffs, NJ: Prentice Hall.

Walton, J. (1999). *Strategic Human Resource Development.* London, U.K.: Financial Times Management/Prentice Hall.

About the Authors

■ ■

Donald V. McCain

As founder and principal of Performance Advantage Group, Donald McCain has dedicated the organization to helping companies gain competitive advantage through the development of their human resources. With more than 28 years of corporate and consulting experience, McCain's focus is on design and development of custom learning experiences in leadership, sales and marketing, call center management, and many areas of professional development that result in improved business unit and individual performance.

He also consults in HRD processes, including design/development, competency identification and development, certification, evaluation (including transfer and return-on-investment), presentation and facilitation, and managing and marketing the HRD function. Most of his clients are *Fortune* 100 companies across various industries. His work is international in scope. McCain has also consulted with many new consultants on the business side of training consulting.

McCain has a bachelor's degree in business administration, a master's degree of divinity, a master's degree of business administration with a concentration in HR and marketing, and a doctorate in education in HRD from Vanderbilt University. He is a member of ASTD and the American Management Association International (AMAI), and a former member of the Academy of Human Resource Development (AHRD). McCain previously served as an adjunct assistant professor of leadership and organizations for Vanderbilt University and is currently an adjunct professor for the school of management at Belmont University. He also teaches for the University of Phoenix.

He is author of the book *Creating Training Courses (When You're Not A Trainer)* (ASTD, 1999) and also wrote the lead article for *HRfocus*, "Aligning Training With

Business Objectives" (February, 1999). Additionally, he has published several evaluation instruments.

He lives in Nashville, Tennessee, with his wife Kathy and their two boys, Weston and Colin. He also has two married daughters, Kimberly and Karla. Donald McCain may be contacted at donpag@bellsouth.net.

Deborah Davis Tobey

Building on her nearly 20 years' experience in the field, Deborah Davis Tobey is principal of Deb Tobey LLC, a consulting practice in human and organization performance improvement. She works with client organizations in consulting skills development and consulting systems; training needs assessment, design, facilitation, and evaluation; strategic planning; teambuilding; group process consultation; competency modeling; and leadership development. Her clients include *Fortune* 500 organizations in manufacturing, finance, import, health care, the service sector, as well as nonprofit organizations, state and local governments, and universities.

Tobey functions often in a mentor/coaching role with HRD professionals and students. She has served ASTD in several officer capacities for 10 years.

She has a bachelor's degree in English and a master's degree in student personnel administration and counseling from Virginia Tech. Her doctorate in HRD is from Vanderbilt University. She served for four years as adjunct professor of the practice in HRD at Vanderbilt University and is currently an adjunct professor in the HRD graduate program at George Washington University.

Tobey is author/creator of several proprietary tools and processes that assist her clients: The EchoSource Consulting Skills Model, which helps consultants assess their clients and develop strategies that match the client's needs; HRD Frameworking, a coaching process that assists HRD internal consultants in developing and strengthening the expertise in their units; and Outcome Processing, a data reduction process that assists clients in gathering and making meaning of data so that it can be used as a strategic planning input.

She lives in Nashville, Tennessee, with her husband, Bryan Tobey. Deborah Davis Tobey may be reached at dtobey@mindspring.com or www.debtobey.com.

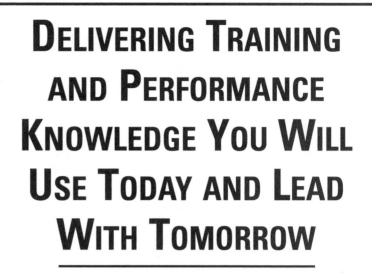